Winning Bowling

Earl Anthony
with Dawson Taylor

CB
CONTEMPORARY
BOOKS
CHICAGO

Library of Congress Cataloging-in-Publication Data

Anthony, Earl, 1938–
    Winning bowling / Earl Anthony and Dawson Taylor.
       p.   cm.
    Includes index.
    ISBN 0-8092-3526-9
    1. Bowling.   I. Taylor, Dawson.   II. Title.
GV903.A56   1994
794.6—dc20   94-21344
                                        CIP

Photographs by Jerry Gay

Copyright © 1994, 1977 by Earl Anthony and Dawson Taylor
All rights reserved
Published by Contemporary Books, Inc.
Two Prudential Plaza, Chicago, Illinois 60601-6790
Manufactured in the United States of America
International Standard Book Number: 0-8092-3526-9
10   9   8   7   6   5   4   3   2   1

To Marylou, Mike, Jeri, and Tracy Anthony
To Mary Ellen, Denise, Christine, and Dawson Taylor

Contents

Note to the Reader

Bowling fans know that Earl Anthony is left-handed. It may come as a surprise to them to see that in the many photographs in this book, he seems to be a right-hander. Not so, however. The photographs were all shot with Earl operating left-handed, and by a photographic practice called "flopping the negative" he is made to appear to be bowling right-handed, as do most bowlers. Incidentally, no action pictures were posed. Balls were rolled for all photos showing bowling action.

Bowling has many technical terms, many of them otherwise ordinary words, such as strike, spare, frame, but with special meanings for bowling. Where such terms appear for the first time, we have tried to clear their meaning. A glossary at the end of the book repeats these terms, in case we missed any, or the reader forgets.

CHAPTER 1

My name is Earl Anthony. I am 39 years old and live in Tacoma, Washington, with my family: Marylou, my wife; my three children, Mike, 17 years old, Jeri, 19 years old, Tracy, 14 years old; and Puff, the dog.

When Marylou and I were first married we had no idea that I would ever earn our living by bowling. I used to work for a wholesale grocery company on the midnight shift. I didn't earn a lot of money and sometimes it was hard to make ends meet, especially when the children started coming along.

For recreation, I used to play baseball. I had been in the Air Force before I was married and really like to pitch, and especially to bat. I think you might say I was a good ball player but certainly not good enough to consider a professional career.

How I Got Started in Bowling

I had never bowled in my life until I was 21. Soon after I started to work for the grocery company, I found out that there was a company bowling league. I was invited to join it. So I did. Bowling was rather expensive. I felt a little guilty about telling Marylou I was going to bowl "with the boys."

Because I worked the graveyard shift, I bowled early in the morning. Right after work we'd have a bite of breakfast and be on the lanes by 9 A.M. Sometimes I'd be tired, but mostly I was still wide-awake from the night's physical activity of moving cases of food around and keeping busy lining up loads for the trucks to deliver in the early morning.

In my first bowling season, I averaged about 165. That was not bad for a beginner, but it wasn't good enough to win any pot games from the better bowlers of the league. In pot games, every bowler puts a certain amount in the pot, and winner takes all. I was attracted to the game, and although I was sort of an oddity because I threw the bowling ball left-handed, it didn't really bother me to be kidded. I just resolved to improve my bowling as much as I could.

So I started practicing bowling whenever I got the chance. I knew a friendly alley owner, and he would often let me roll a few games in return for my setting up the pins for a certain number of games. This was before the automatic pin setters came into use, of course. Then, too, I found that I could "shadow bowl" and learn a great deal about bowling. Shadow bowling, I am sure you know, is the practice of bowling at imaginary pins, that is rolling the ball down an empty lane.

I was trying to perfect my timing and my footwork. I found that by shadow bowling I could concentrate more completely on the bowling problem I was having at that time, too fast a first step, an irregular approach when I zigzagged instead of going straight to the foul line, and especially my timing so that the ball would be in a position alongside my sliding foot in every delivery.

I would sometimes shadow bowl 25 to 30 games a day. It was much less expensive, of course, and really it proved to be most effective in improving my bowling style. Sometimes I would trade the alley owner a clean-up job on his pins for letting me shadow bowl on an otherwise unused lane.

My bowling started to improve dramatically. In one year, my average had gone into the middle 180's, and in one more year, I was in the low 200's. Bowlers who had been beating me regularly before were now finding that "the left-hander"was taking their money most of the time.

Marylou was a little happier, too, about my bowling expenses. She was really very tolerant and encouraged me all the way. And, as I got into bigger and bigger pot games, I was bringing home more and more "pin" money for her, I began to consider becoming a professional bowler.

At last the opportunity came for me to prove to myself whether I could make it as a professional bowler. One of the professional bowling tour events came to our area. Amateurs are invited to compete in these events. As a matter of fact, their entries are substantial and help the professional bowlers' treasury a great deal. I bowled with the bowlers who were acknowledged to be the best in the world. I was surprised to find that I could not only keep up with them, but when the event was ended, I found that although I finished out of the money I had out-bowled more than a hundred other very good bowlers.

That planted a seed in my mind. I began to think that maybe I could make it as a professional bowler and earn enough money to support my family. It would be risky, I knew, but I had then, as I do now, a great deal of confidence in my ability not only to bowl well but also, and this is even more important, to bowl well under pressure. I had seasoned in those pot games and was able to produce the crucial final strikes I needed. Furthermore, some special secrets of bowling that I had uncovered in my thousands of games of shadow bowling and league games were paying off. I felt that I was on the brink of a break through in bowling style...and I was.

What I had discovered about bowling style would help me to become the top Professional Bowler of the Year in 1974, 1975, and 1976 and earn a record $110,785 in prize money in one single year. Then I decided that I would attempt to pass on to the other bowlers of America, possibly even of the world, some of the things that I have observed during my extensive career. I decided that if I wrote a book of instruction on bowling I would emphasize the fundamentals of bowling technique and try to make my instructions so clear that someone who had never put on a pair of bowling shoes in his life nor rolled a bowling ball would come away after reading my observations with a complete understanding of the bowling game. For it is a game. It is great fun to knock down those pins 60 feet away at the end of the lane, and the more you knock them down the more you become addicted to the bowling game.

It is now 1994. My book *Winning Bowling* has been a success for more than 17 years. I am most gratified and would like to express my appreciation to Contemporary Books for realizing the necessity of bringing *Winning Bowling* up-to-date.

First of all, I should tell you, the reader, about my bowling career subsequent to the first publication of *Winning Bowling* in 1977. I continued to bowl most successfully on the Professional Bowling Tour and won 32 championships, bringing my total to 41, more than any other bowler in history. I earned more than $2 million in prize money and endorsements. I also suffered a heart attack along the way—from which, I am pleased to say, I have made a successful recovery.

But the time came for me to slow down, so recently I went into semiretirement. I now live in the beautiful countryside near Tacoma, Washington. I hunt, fish, and play golf. My golf game has improved to the point that I now score in the mid-70's. An oddity is that while I always bowled left-handed, I play golf right-handed.

I keep busy in the bowling world by commentating on television bowling programs. In that way I have also kept up with all the changes and improvements in the world of bowling.

Nearly all the improvements and changes in bowling techniques relate to the improved manufacture of bowling balls. Computers and the plastics industry have combined to produce bowling balls that will give the ordinary bowler practically any type of strike action he or she wants. This may vary from a gentle, persistent curve into the 1-3 pocket to a ball that hurtles down the lane barely missing the right channel and then "flips" sideways into the 1-3 pocket, smashing the pins against the left-hand side so that they rocket across the lane taking out the 10-pin and producing a guaranteed strike.

You will find the latest information about these improved bowling balls in the next chapter, "Let's Go Bowling."

CHAPTER 2

When you first take an interest in bowling, if you are like millions of other Americans, it happens this way. One of your friends suggests, "Let's go bowling!" And because you don't want to admit you are a novice, reluctantly you say "Yes." From then on, you are hooked on one of the greatest participant sports in America.

Your neighborhood bowling lanes provide your first bowling ball, what is known as a "house ball," one of a great number of bowling balls available for customers who don't own their own. You try your fingers in countless finger holes and at last find a ball that seems to fit your hand and does not stretch your fingers too much. Then the bowling counterman asks you your shoe size, and you find yourself rattling around in a strange pair of bowling shoes a half-size too large.

Let's Go Bowling

You have just been introduced to the basic equipment of bowling. As you bowl, you come to realize that some of the other bowlers on the lanes, perhaps even sharing the ball rack and benches with you, own their own bowling balls, bowling shoes, and bags, in which they carry their own ball, shoes, and a few other things we will get to later.

If you are going to bowl seriously, you should most certainly have your own bowling equipment: ball, bag, and shoes. Many bowling pro-shops have all kinds of such equipment and sometimes will package those three items in a sale. With the proper hinting, you might even get your husband or wife to give them to you as a birthday or Christmas present.

If you were going to have a serious brain operation, you would insist that the best brain surgeon perform the operation, wouldn't you? Well, while the choice of a new bowling ball is not quite so serious a matter as brain surgery, the best suggestion I can give you on your choice and proper fit of a new bowling ball is to have the best bowling "doctor" diagnose your bowling situation.

In every big city there is a specialist in drilling bowling balls. The good bowlers all know who he is; so ask a good bowler who drills the balls for the best bowlers in your town. Often times there is more than one, for just as some people prefer one doctor to another, some bowlers swear by one ball-drilling specialist and some rave about another. The good bowler might recommend your own local bowling proprietor himself.

My advice is that you find the best ball-drilling specialist and put yourself in his hands. If a certain house ball has felt good to you, ask the proprietor if you might borrow it for a little while. He'll probably allow you to do so. Take it with you to the specialist. His measuring devices will tell him what length of span there should be between your thumb and your third and fourth fingers. At first, he will probably drill for you what is called a conventional ball, that is, a ball fitted to the first joint of your fingers from the palm. He will know to provide for the proper pitch, or angle, to allow your thumb to get out of the ball comfortably. He will bevel the outer edges of the finger holes smooth so that they won't cause unnecessary wear on your fingers as they come out of the ball.

In the early days of bowling, before there were weight and balance limitations on bowling balls, bowlers found that putting extra weights on one side of the ball or the other created a devastating wobbling effect as the ball hit the pins. That's why the rules were changed to control and standardize the weight and other characteristics of the ball. But a slightly out-of-balance ball is permissible, and it allows the modern bowler to take advantage of the odd physical action occurring at the pins when a ball that is legally top-weighted, side-weighted, or finger-weighted hits them.

As you bowl under differing lane conditions, as I have done

all my bowling life, you will discover that lanes will differ from extremely slick, or fast, on which your ball will hardly hook (move from right to left) at all, to extremely running, or slow, on which it is difficult to keep your ball from running (head on) into the headpin (1 pin) or else crossing over into the left, or Brooklyn, side (between the 1 and 2 pins).

I have found that it is possible to balance my bowling ball so that it snaps into the pocket (the space between the 1 and 3 pins) as strong, stronger, and strongest. The difference is probably two or three degrees of increased hook as the ball enters the pocket. With the strong, stronger, and strongest balls, I use the strongest ball on stiff alleys; the stronger one on normal alleys; and the strong one, of course, on the running or hooking lanes. Lane conditions vary so much that I cannot set down for you any simple rule as to which ball is best, but in any case you will have only one ball at first, and you will have to compensate in other ways that we will discover later.

While these are my own personal ball balances that give me a "strong," "stronger," and "strongest" ball, it is imperative that you have confidence in your own local ball-driller and ball-balancer and let him work with you to achieve your own personal balances for your bowling balls. In general, if you roll a "spinner" you should not have top balance, but what is called "zero" balance or a ball that is close to being perfectly balanced. In general, if you roll a full-roller you should add top weight to your ball. I wish that I could give you specific balances but that is impossible in view of the fact that everyone, including the professional bowlers themselves, roll their balls with different hand action. Some release the ball "softly" so the roll starts early, some late and the roll starts later.

I do advise you that if you find a ball-balance that gives you a "strong" ball in hooking action at the pocket, somewhere along the line there are two other drillings and balances that will give you the "stronger" and "strongest" ball for yourself. Be patient. Work with your alley manager and develop a consistent ball with consistent roll and hooking action. It is well worth the trouble and will pay off in increased strike action for you.

Now that you have your very own first bowling ball; and since you are in the hands of the specialist, don't be afraid to come back to him and say, "That third finger hole seems a little tight. The ball is hanging on it." He has the knowledge and skill to adjust the ball so that it fits perfectly. It must fit perfectly.

Here is my advice about ball balance. Trust that specialist to balance the ball for you. He will ask you where your ball rolls, or tracks, most of the time. Your answer to this question is important because it indicates to him where he should put the top, side, and finger weight on your ball. The American Bowling Congress (ABC) realizes that it is a physical impossibility to manufacture a bowling ball in absolutely perfect dynamic balance. So the rules of the ABC provide that a bowling ball may be out of balance by no more than a few ounces according to a definite mathematical formula.*

There are bowling aids that I suggest you have available in your bowling bag and use occasionally. The first is rosin, available at most bowling establishment counters in a little jar impregnated in beeswax. Just a tiny dab on your fingertips will help to keep them dry and enable you to grip the ball more firmly. A small can of talcum powder is a good thing to have, too, for a drying agent if you perspire abnormally. You must be very careful not to get talcum on the lanes, however, because it will make any spot it falls on very slippery.

You should also buy and keep in your bowling bag a small

---

* The American Bowling Congress rules for bowling ball specifications require that: "Bowling balls shall be so constructed and drilled that no less than six sides shall be in proper balance. The following tolerances shall be permissible in the balance of a bowling ball:

   10 pounds or more—
        a. Not more than 3 ounces difference between the top of ball (finger hole side) and the bottom (solid side opposite finger holes).
        b. Not more than 1 ounce difference between the sides to the right and left of the finger holes or between the sides in front and back of the finger holes."

And recently the ABC has instituted the rule that the "surface hardness of bowling balls shall not be less than 72 Durometer 'D'" (a reference to a hardness testing device).

bottle of collodion and a small roll of cotton for the protection of a sore or rubbed spot on a finger. There is a real art in applying this type of bandage. You should practice when you really do not need it in order to be ready for the awful situation when you do need it. The collodion is spread on the blistered or rubbed spot and a very thin layer of cotton is laid on top of it while the collodion is still wet. As the collodion hardens, it forms a durable surface over the sore spot. It is truly a lifesaver for many bowlers.

If you find that you must dope your fingers frequently in this way, however, your bowling ball probably does not fit you properly. Get some expert advice from a good bowling professional or a good ball-driller, and you may be able to avoid the problem in the future merely by a slight change in the drilling of your ball.

I also recommend that you carry in your bowling bag at all times a small packet of steel wool. You will use this on the sole of your shoe for the sliding foot in the event that the sole picks up some foreign substance such as gum or floor wax that might interfere with your normal smooth slide. Along this same line, good bowlers make a habit of checking their sliding soles every time they bowl. Practice your slide at the front of the approach before you bowl. You may save yourself a nasty spill! If the left shoe has picked up some water on its sole and the bowler proceeds to bowl not knowing about the water, he is apt to cause himself a serious injury because the wet sole acts on the approach surface as a sudden brake. And don't forget an extra pair of shoelaces for your shoes. There is nothing more likely to create panic than having a broken shoelace and no replacement just as you are preparing to bowl an important game!

BOWLING GRIPS

There are three common grips in bowling today, the conventional grip, the fingertip grip, and the semi-fingertip grip. It is odd to think that in the early days of bowling there were no finger-holes in the bowling balls. The bowlers held the ball in the palm of the hand and rolled it that way.

I recommend the conventional grip for the average bowler and especially for the beginning bowler. This grip gives the most solid feeling of having something to hang onto, something that can be controlled and will not slip out of the hand. The drilling for this grip is such that the finger holes are drilled beneath the break of the first joints of the third and fourth fingers of your bowling hand. The thumb hole is drilled to accept the full length of the thumb, and the other two holes allow the other two fingers to have from one-half to two-thirds of the fingerhole touching the fingers, with the same space left at the back of the fingers. There should be a snug fit for all the fingers and yet one that allows the fingers to get out of the ball without unnecessary drag or friction. The ball-driller uses pitch, or angle, in the drilling so as to give the bowler the feeling of clutching his fingers around a substantial object. The finger holes cannot be too snug or they will create a vacuum that will exert undesirable drag as the fingers leave the ball.

BALL-FITTING AND BALL-DRILLING

For many years in the early days of bowling there was a complete lack of understanding of how important it is that each bowler have his own bowling ball drilled with finger holes that fit his fingers properly and that those holes be spaced on the bowling ball and drilled at certain angles in such a manner that the bowler could execute a good release of the ball out over the foul line (the line on or beyond which the bowler's person cannot encroach so that it touches the lane, as, say, the sliding foot).

Over the last several decades, there has been a great deal of study on the best ways to drill and fit bowling balls with the result that certain individuals with great patience and understanding in addition to imagination and knowledge of the bowling ball's "gyroscopic inertia" factor have become experts in their localities, much sought after as "doctors" of bowling trouble, whether it be sore fingers or the inability to control the release of the ball.

Consider what the bowler is trying to accomplish with each bowling delivery—a smooth, rhythmic movement of the body, bowling arm, and bowling ball into a forward stride that will take the bowler's body to the delivery point at the foul line as the bottom of the descending arc of the bowling ball in its forward swing reaches the point of release. Remember that the ball with its 16 pounds of weight is developing a very powerful centrifugal force in itself.

The delivery will be faulty if the bowler is not in the proper physical position as the ball reaches its delivery point. The delivery will also be faulty if the bowler is unable to hang onto the ball, that is, has a finger grip which costs him control by either "hanging up," or retaining the thumb, for too long a time. Or the delivery will be faulty if the reverse is true: if the thumb or either or both of the other fingers release early and thus drop the ball.

So the objective of a proper ball fit is to insure the ability of the bowler to make a suitable release of the ball. In fact it should be not only a suitable release, but the most perfect release of the ball, consistently frame after frame.

The release of the thumb from the bowling ball is the most important part of the delivery of the ball. The thumb must come out no sooner and no later than the exact fraction of a second of time which will allow the fingers to continue in the ball and impart the lift, or action, on the ball. If the thumb hole is too loose or slanted in too great a reverse pitch, the thumb may come out too soon so that the fingers cannot do their work. If the thumb hole is too tight, the ball may "hang up" on the bowler's thumb; and even if the fingers are ready to put their effect on the ball, they cannot do so.

You know that I cannot try on your new shoes for you, nor

can you fit mine. Each one of us has a different body with different lengths of arms and sizes of hands and fingers. I want you to take my advice in this matter. It is derived from years of experimentation on my own part and by others in the search for the perfectly drilled bowling ball. My advice to you is this: Go to the best ball-driller you can find in your own bowling backyard. Have confidence in him. Tell him your problems. Show him your sore fingertips or swollen thumb. He will work with you and, if you are patient, you will eventually possess a truly personalized drilled bowling ball, tailored to fit your style of delivery.

Purely as a matter of interest, my personal drillings are as follows: thumb, $1\frac{1}{16}$ in. with a $\frac{1}{4}$ inch reverse pitch; third finger, $\frac{3}{4}$ in. and second finger, $\frac{13}{16}$ in., with no pitch. For my strong ball, the weightings are $\frac{1}{2}$ oz. side and 1 oz. top; the stronger ball, $\frac{1}{2}$ oz. side and finger, and $1\frac{1}{2}$ oz. top; the strongest ball, 1 oz. side and finger, and $2\frac{1}{2}$ oz. top.

THE REACTIVE RESIN REVOLUTION

The plastic called urethane was introduced into the manufacture of bowling balls about twenty-five years ago. At first it was used primarily as a new outer shell surface material. As technology advanced the manufacturers realized that with denser outer shells and slightly off-balance inner cores they could make the ball "do tricks." So, after much experimentation the Reactive Resin ball was invented. It has a larger volume high-density core which produces a heavy, predictable roll with the greatest amount of "snap" in the backends into the 1-3 pocket.

All the manufacturers are making Reactive Resin balls. They are more expensive and cost in the neighborhood of $150. However, the results they achieve are nothing less than sensational.

The drilling of such a ball for a bowler is extremely precise. In the next paragraph, for example, are the instructions for the drilling of an AMF bowling ball that will "produce a strong hook with a late break point and a sharp hook angle." The drilling produces a large track flare, too. That is, the ball will go out a long way toward the channel and then return to the pocket.

The ball-driller must rotate the ball so the pin (top of the ball) is at the 12 o'clock position in relation to the center of gravity. The ball-driller must place the pin exactly $3\frac{3}{8}$ inches from the positive axis point on the ball and place the center of gravity at the proper position in relation to the midline to achieve the desired finger or thumb weight. The weight hole (a drilling of an open hole to bring the ball into conformity with ABC regulations on ball balance) is to be placed 2 inches beyond the positive axis point on the midline to achieve the desired side weight.

This information is extremely complicated and understandable only to an experienced ball-driller, of course, but the very complexity of these instructions makes them interesting.

Please take my recommendation that you consult the best ball-driller in your area and have confidence that he will drill you a bowling ball that will suit your delivery.

Here Mike LaMeyer, a certified bowling coach, points out the asymmetrical bowling ball cores that are now in use in the Reactive Resin balls. It is the off-center weight that causes the tremendous snap into the 1-3 pocket at the end of the lane.

CHAPTER 3

WHAT WE ARE TRYING TO DO

Shown on p. 18 is a diagram of the bowling pin set-up, the target of your bowling ball. On each of these spots, stands a bowling pin of not less than three pounds and two ounces nor more than three pounds and ten ounces in weight. That is a total weight of more than 31 pounds. Each bowling pin stands 15 inches high and is a little more than 4½ inches in diameter at its widest part. The pins are set in a 36 inch triangle. The center of each pin is one foot from the centers of each nearest pin.

The first thing you must understand is the obvious disparity in asking a round ball weighing 16 pounds or less to roll down a lane slightly longer than 60 feet and by striking the first two of those pins, knock all of them down for what is called a strike. There is a mathematical answer and I will show you before we

The Grip

have finished how it is done. The answer lies in giving the bowling ball the proper angle (the imaginary line from the ball as it comes on the lane to the point at which it strikes between the 1 and 3 pins) as it enters the bowling pin set up and in putting action (movement imparted to the ball by the fingers as the ball is released) on the ball as it does so.

The first thing a bowler does is to pick up his ball from the bowling rack. Two of the illustrations on the next page show the right way and the wrong way to pick up a bowling ball from the rack. Always put your hands on the sides of the ball in such a way that another ball returning cannot cause a ball jam and catch your fingers between the two balls. As soon as you pick the ball up, begin to support it with your non-bowling arm and hand so as to lessen the strain on your bowling arm and hand.

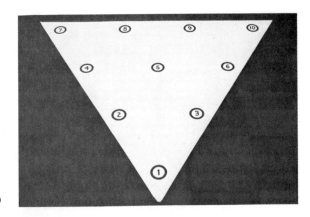

Set-up

The right way to pick up a bowling ball

The wrong way to pick up a bowling ball

18

THE GRIP

In the proper grip, as shown below, the fingers are firm, but relaxed. The wrist is firm. The hand is on the side of the ball with the thumb, as shown, pointing to what would be 10 o'clock on a clock dial. This thumb position will vary from bowler to bowler depending upon the desired action on the bowling ball. But, in general, the thumb will point no farther up than to 11 o'clock and no farther down than to 9 o'clock. The ball is supported partially by the left hand and arm as the right hand and arm prepare to drop the ball away into its backswing.

The proper grip

I bowl with a "fingertip" ball, that is a ball drilled not so deep as a conventional ball, which has finger holes drilled to admit the fingers only to the first joint. Here is the way I take my grip on the ball (below). First, I insert my third and fourth fingers and locate them at the exact depth in the ball I want them to be. My fingerholes are drilled to the precise depths I want so that there can be very little variance from grip to grip. I recommend that you have your ball drilled the same way. Next, I place my thumb in the ball in very relaxed fashion. I recommend that you follow the same procedure. You might even rehearse your thumb release ahead of time to make sure you get your thumb out of the ball and impart action on it.

19

CHAPTER 4

Each bowler takes his stance on the approach to the lane at a different distance, depending on the length of his stride and whether he uses a four-step or a five-step delivery, which we will discuss later. The approach has three sets of dots across it, one near the foul line (separating the lane from the approach). If a bowler will put his heel on the approach side of the foul line and take four steps and a half (for the four-step delivery), the half to allow for his slide as he completes his approach, he will find an approximate starting point. Two more rows of dots at the back of the approach indicate approximate starting points for the four-step and five-step deliveries. Each bowler will adjust to his best starting point by trial-and-error, of course.

On p. 22 is my stance, the one I advocate for most bowlers. My eyes are fixed on my target out on the lane. My ball is held toward the side of my body so that it can drop away in a

The Stance

smooth pendulum arc into its backswing. My body feels square, that is at a right angle, to my intended line, the path I imagine the ball will follow to the pins. My knees are slightly flexed, relaxed, not stiff. My feet are close to each other so as to aid me in a smooth straight approach to the foul line. Note the concentration of my eyes on the intended spot on the lane. I will take one deep breath, exhale, relax, and go!

THE DROPAWAY AND THE PUSHAWAY

Each bowler must find his own personal method of beginning the bowling procedure. I will call it the ball-step move in order to emphasize in your mind the importance of understanding that the first movement of the body toward the foul line and the first

My stance

movement of the ball and arm must coincide consistently every time in order for the bowler to achieve his desired result: the proper timing of the bottom of the arc of the bowling ball and the arm to coincide with the sliding foot at the foul line.

I prefer to use what I call a dropaway start for my bowling sequence. If you will observe my bowling style, you will see that I hold the ball with most of the weight taken up by the non-bowling hand and arm. For me it is my right, for you, the right-handed bowler, it is your left. Since I have found that my method of the ball-step move works for me, I would like to recommend that you learn it, too.

I will agree that it does take some hand and arm strength to hold the ball in its forward position in front of the body and slightly to the side. But I believe that with practice and with the aid of some of the hand and arm-strengthening exercises that I will talk about later, you will be able to duplicate my motions.

I think it is a good way to start because there are no false moves in it, no complications. I put the ball out there in front of me at the forward point of its arc and when I am ready to take my first step, I just let the ball drop away with its own weight helping to carry it down and backward in the bowling arc.

MY DROPAWAY

This is a view of my start from overhead. I take my first step (here marked for demonstration purposes on the floor beneath my supporting hand) and then drop the ball away into its pendulum arc. That moment *coincides exactly* with the second step of my five-step delivery. In a four-step delivery it must coincide with the first step. If this action is consistently timed, 90 percent of your troubles in timing are over.

THE PUSHAWAY

Here (below) Dawson Taylor demonstrates one of the two acceptable ways of starting your delivery, the pushaway. With the ball close to the chest, the first move is to push it away straight forward at the exact second the right foot makes its move toward the foul line. The weight is back on the left heel so that there is no interruption of the rhythmic step forward by the right foot. The stance is fairly upright, and is relaxed by a slight flexing of the knees. Both hips and shoulders are squared (that is perpendicular) to the intended line of the ball, from the foul line through the arrows (dart-like markers) on the lane.

The pushaway

THE DROPAWAY

Here (below) Dawson Taylor demonstrates the other acceptable method of starting the bowling delivery, the dropaway. The ball is held out at the end of the bowling arm in a position from which it can drop away smoothly into its downward arc in the backswing. In this delivery, too, there should be relaxation in the knees, a fairly upright stance, and the feeling of squareness to the intended line or "track" of the ball from the foul line through the arrows on the lane.

The dropaway

THE FIRST MOVE

You may not be able to copy my dropaway start with the ball. If not, don't worry! There are many other variations of the start, many of them just as effective as mine. So you probably will be able to work out for yourself one of the following variations.

Often, you will see a true pushaway of the ball at the start of a bowler's stride. In this variation you will notice that the bowler holds the ball fairly close to his midsection, sometimes at his chest, and pushes the ball forward with his first step. That's why this style or start is called a pushaway. There is nothing wrong with it provided that the bowler is able to achieve the proper timing of the arc of the ball to the sliding foot as we have explained before. Sometimes the bowler who uses the pushaway start does not push the ball out to exactly the same distance time after time. Obviously, if the arc of the ball is shortened or lengthened an inch one time and not the next time, there are going to be inconsistencies in the bowler's approach and delivery, inconsistencies which may result in irregular bowling, good, bad, and indifferent from game to game.

I believe that the more mechanical I can make my delivery, the more consistently repetitive from first step on through the completion of my full body and arm follow-through after the ball is on its way down the lane, the better I will score, the better I *do* score.

I am also of the opinion that it is wise to help the ball get into its proper arc by placing it there ahead of time. You will notice, I am sure, that just as many other good bowlers do, I place the ball slightly to one side of my body so that when it falls away in the downswing, it is already in the proper arc. There should be no necessity for the ball to find the bowler's body in the way as it starts into the downswing.

I have noticed, and I am sure that you have, too, that some bowlers hold the ball in a spot directly in front of their middles, or at the belt-buckle position. I believe that by doing so the bowler is apt to cause the bowling ball arc to go outside his body and thus cause any one of several bad results later on at the foul line as he attempts to deliver the ball. He will leave the ball in an outside position from which he can only deliver it across his intended line; or else, instinctively realizing that he has put the ball outside, he will attempt to correct the situation by bringing the ball and his arm around behind his body—all of which will result in a poor delivery and inconsistent bowling. Remember: "Keep it simple, keep it timed, keep it rhythmic— stay down at the line, and *follow through!*"

SQUARENESS TO YOUR BOWLING LINE

I cannot emphasize too greatly the importance of your understanding and accomplishing what I call squareness to the bowling line as you deliver your bowling ball out over the foul line.

You will remember in my discussion of setting yourself for your first step that I told you how you must feel that your body is square, that is, at a right angle to your intended bowling line. By this I mean that you should have the feeling that if a line were drawn from right to left through your upper chest and a similar line drawn through your hips they would be perfectly parallel to the foul line. At the same time, you should feel that those lines are at a perfect right angle to your intended bowling line, which you should see in your mind's eye as a line running directly down the lane from your starting spot at the foul line through the second range finder (or arrow) out on the lane. I want you to be patient with me in this discussion of squareness. Later on I will explain to you how this squareness to the line is applied to a bowling line which does not go straight down the lane but goes out toward the channel (the gutter on each side of the lane) at first, and then returns to hit the pocket (the space between the 1-pin and the 3-pin).

CHAPTER 5

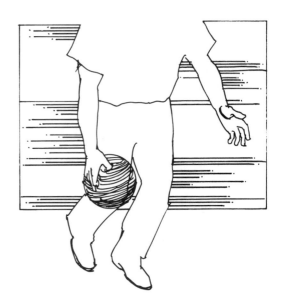

The first step is taken as you perform your dropaway or pushaway. You step off with your right foot (your left if you are left-handed). The first step is short, nearly a half step. The ball as it falls into position for the backswing helps to move your weight forward, carrying you into the next step.

THE FOUR-STEP DELIVERY

The proper footwork for a four-step delivery is shown on p. 30. In spite of how it looks from the camera angle, these steps are all of the same length. I prefer to see them all in the same tempo, too, that is,

The Delivery

evenly paced rather than accelerated after the first step. The last step may appear to be a longer one because of the slide, but it really is not. Be sure that your last step finds you with bent knee sliding straight ahead. In that way you will be able to follow through straight up with your hand, arm, and shoulder as you deliver the ball out over the foul line. Although I personally use a five-step delivery, I advocate the four-step delivery for most bowlers. The five-step delivery, is in my opinion, nothing more than a four step delivery with a little beginning move to eliminate tension. In either delivery the movement of the bowling ball into its downswing should coincide exactly with the fourth from the last step.

Now I want you to concentrate on your hand position as the subject for the second fundamental in the bowling swing. While

Four-step delivery

standing in bowling starting position, I want you to be able to look down at your hand as it is placed inside the ball and visualize your third and fourth fingers in a slightly hooked, curled, tensed position inside the ball and see your thumb pointing on an axis from 5 o'clock at its root to 11 o'clock at its tip. The back of your hand is flat and the line along it and back up your wrist is a straight line, as in the photo of the proper grip.

I want you to attempt to visualize this finger position as being held all the way through your downswing and your forward swing right on through the moment of release of the bowling ball. In order to accomplish this hand position I have found, and you will find also as you practice doing it, that it is necessary for there to be a slight counterclockwise rotation of the hand as it proceeds downward and backward. As you perform this physical maneuver, you will also note that the weight of the ball remains in the fingers, which is exactly what I want you to accomplish.

Do not worry about how far you carry this finger action in the backswing. As your bowling style develops you will naturally reach the best possible stopping point in your backswing, the one that will be most natural for you.

The 4-Step Delivery
The Second Fundamental

There should not be any breaking of your wrist to the side, flattening as it is called. If you find that this happens in spite of your desire not to have it happen, it may be caused by any one of several problems.

First, your ball may be too heavy for you to handle comfortably. Second, your wrist may be weak and need strengthening exercises (See Chapter 16 for bowling exercises). Third, the fit of your ball to your fingers may be incorrect, the span may be too wide for you, thus forcing your hand and wrist to break either downward or to the side.

THE FIVE-STEP DELIVERY

In my opinion, the five-step delivery is nothing more than a four-step delivery with a forward press of the first step as the delivery actually accomplishes the rhythm and timing of the four-step delivery, that is, with the ball starting into its backswing in coincidence with the second step of the five-step approach. The forward press brings about a relaxation for some bowlers. If it works for you, you should try it. I recommend that you start out with the four-step delivery, however, and stick with it as long as it works for you.

The Third Step

With the third step of the five-step delivery (which would be the second step of a four-step delivery), the ball is dropping away into its backswing and the left foot is making its straight approach to the foul line. Note that the hand position (without the ball so that position is clear) remains the same as it was when the ball was dropped away, with the thumb on the inside, the fingers firm on the outside, the wrist flat, straight and unbroken.

With the fourth step, the bowler goes into his slide and prepares for release of the ball.

Third step of five–step delivery

This view from above shows how I apply leverage to my ball. My left knee is still bent in its slide to the foul line. I am leaning forward and feel that my center of gravity is directly down through my body and my leg pointing at the spot where the ball will be released alongside my sliding foot. I feel completely on balance and ready to lift my bowling ball from behind. It is this lift, which I call leverage, which gives me power on the ball.

Leverage to ball shown in view from above

CHAPTER 6

You have started your slide. Near the end of it comes what I call the moment of truth, the most important split second of your bowling swing at which you release the ball and follow through with your arm and shoulder as the ball leaves your fingers.

Your body has come forward smoothly and then with the application of the brake on your left shoe comes to a smooth stop. The left knee, by remaining bent during the slide on the front part of the sole of your left shoe has kept the heel brake from coming down on the lane until the last part of the slide. The left knee finally straightens, puts the brake down, and at the same time allows the weight of the body to come forward and help to bring the slide to a stop.

The Release

During the arm-swing of the bowling ball, the weight of the ball has been supported for the most part by the thumb with the fingers and wrist lending assistance and control. Now as the ball reaches the bottom of its arc, coming forward in the forward swing as the thumb begins to leave the ball first, the weight of the ball starts to transfer from the bowler's thumb to the bowler's fingers. There is a fraction of a second during which the fingers alone are carrying the ball and it is this moment that I call the moment of truth in the bowler's game.

At this point any letdown or failure of the fingers to act in proper fashion will "kill the ball," or at least cause it to have less action on it than the bowler desires. At this moment of truth the thumb should be pointing toward the center of the ball. At the

35

foul line this means that the thumb is pointing straight toward the floor at the bottom of the pendulum swing; and as the ball is released out over the foul line, the thumb, although now out of the ball completely, remains pointing straight toward the bowler's target.

Remember that in order to roll a natural hook ball the fingers must remain on the right-hand side of the ball throughout the release of the ball and, most important of all, must never pass a 3 o'clock position on the side of the ball for fear of "overturning," or reversing the proper finger action.

THE TWO PROPER STYLES OF BALL RELEASE: WITHOUT WRIST TURN AND WITH WRIST TURN

There are, of course, literally hundreds of ways to release the bowling ball at the foul line. But you will notice that the title reads "proper" styles of ball release.

You will also see a great many trick finger positions, too: positions that start this delivery, even to the sight of the fingers in front and on top of the ball at 12 o'clock or 1 o'clock on a clock dial and the thumb tending backward toward 8 o'clock. Carmen Salvino is noted for such a trick grip, and it has been remarkably effective for him over years of bowling.

In my opinion there are basically two methods of ball release that lead to effective strong bowling ball action. The first one, without wrist turn, I consider to be the natural ball many bowlers roll. This is the kind of delivery in which there is no effort on the part of the bowler to impart additional twist to the ball at the last second in the delivery. I do not like to define this ball in negative fashion, but the truth of the matter is that it must be described as something it is not.

With the natural no wrist turn release, the bowler takes the ball back in his backswing being careful to keep his thumb inside, that is, on the side of the ball toward his body. In many examples of this delivery there can be seen a distinct counterclockwise turn of the ball as it passes the bowler's side in its downward backswing. This counterclockwise turn should be, in my opinion, only enough to keep the thumb in a position on the side of the ball so that the fingers can remain under the ball and to the right and behind the thumb. I like the thought of the thumb remaining at 10 to 11 o'clock on a clock dial and the fingers at 4 to 5 o'clock, behind the thumb and under the ball. Remember, you never want those fingers to catch up to and pass the thumb in the forward swing; so, if you keep them in the position I suggest during the backswing, they will be in the proper position for the release.

Although what follows is rather technical, please be patient with my explanation. I assure you that in the long run it will be profitable for you.

In the no wrist turn, or natural, release the ball comes forward and the bowler merely lets the physical fact that his thumb is shorter than the fingers and will come out of the ball before the fingers work to provide the split second of time during which the firm tensed fingers, staying in the ball a little longer, lift the ball forward from that behind-the-ball position they have kept all through the swing. Remember that the bowler does not twist or turn his wrist at the moment of the delivery. The bowler's arm and hand come straight up after they have gotten rid of the ball.

Now, for the second style of ball release, with wrist turn. In this type of delivery the bowler may start with his thumb and fingers in much the same positions in the ball as I have advised for the no wrist turn delivery.

The important thing to know about the wrist turn release is that the bowler must get his fingers and thumb into a position on the ball from which, at that last split second, the wrist turn move can be accomplished. This situation usually requires that the bowler start, early or late in his backswing, to get his thumb at about a 12 o'clock position in the ball and his fingers at 6 o'clock. (Sometimes you will see even a 1 o'clock thumb and 7 o'clock finger position.)

These finger and thumb positions must be maintained in the

ball as it comes forward in its downswing and until a second or so before ball release. At that time the wrist is turned violently in counterclockwise fashion. The fingers come from their position behind the ball, the thumb releases at about 10 o'clock (sometimes even 9 o'clock), and then the fingers, continuing in the ball as in the other no wrist turn delivery, impart their own additional lift to the ball in a plane which may be from 4 o'clock to 10 o'clock, from 3 o'clock to 9 o'clock, or any of many variations in between.

I am sure that you can realize from my description of these two types of ball that the natural, no wrist turn delivery is the simpler and easier one to accomplish.

The most important thing to know is that in neither release do the fingers ever get so far forward at the release point that they are ahead of the thumb, as they would be in a 2 o'clock finger, 8 o'clock thumb release.

The no wrist turn natural delivery is the one I recommend for most of my readers. If the wrist turn delivery is a natural one for you, then by all means stick with it and make it work for you. It will take a great deal of practice, but that will be worth it in the long run. It may be frustrating, too, at times because it is considerably more difficult to keep the ball in the pocket with the wrist turn than the no wrist turn delivery. On the other hand, you will often see great strings of devastating strikes when this turned ball is on for the bowler. I repeat that we must work with the tools at hand, our own natural ability, our own differing physiques, and varying strengths of hands, arms, and fingers. Roll the ball that comes most naturally to you and you will prosper in bowling.

I want you to perform a simple experiment in the physics of the bowling ball release. It will work better and more clearly if you can get someone else to help you. Even if you are all alone, however, I want you to demonstrate to yourself why it is so important that the thumb be released from its finger hole before the fingers are released from theirs.

If you are alone, try this: Get an old soft-cushioned chair and place it so that the seat faces you about three or four feet in front of you. Swing the bowling ball in a short swing backward and then forward so as to let the ball go and land on the seat of the chair. Incidentally, make sure the chair is heavy enough and cushioned well enough to take the 16 pound force. You will be able to concentrate on what is happening in your fingers as you make this mock delivery.

If you will keep the back of your hand fairly straight, that is, on a line that continues the line of your forearm on its outer right side, you will observe that the ball must necessarily leave your thumb first, well in advance of leaving the fingers and you will also be aware that this happens primarily because the thumb is shorter than the other fingers. At least it is distinctly shorter than the others when the wrist is held in that straight fashion.

The same experiment can be conducted with another person who catches the ball in mid air as you release it toward him. The trick is really not too difficult to do, but it does take a fairly strong partner, and a brave one, to catch the ball, especially the first time.

I know that if you will perform this action not once but many times, you will have impressed on your mind the proof that you must release the bowling ball in this fashion, with the thumb getting out first and then the fingers continuing to stay with the ball for a second or more as they impart the action to the ball.

You should also be aware that this action of the fingers cannot and will not take place if the ball is dumped, or dropped, near the bowler's foot as it leaves the bowler's hand. It must be delivered out and over the foul line to a certain distance. That distance we will explore when we discuss the action of the ball under varying lane conditions.

Here's another proof exercise for you to try. This time I want you to break your wrist to the right (not downward) so that the thumb is now a continuation of the line on the inside left side of your right arm. The back of your hand and your fingers should now appear to be turned toward 2 o'clock or even 3 o'clock on a clock-dial. (See illustration on page 41.) Now deliver the ball with your hand and wrist in this broken position. The result is that the ball leaves all the fingers more or less simultaneously. Its roll is an end-over-end roll, and there is no chance for side spin, or action, to be imparted to the ball.

Observe other bowlers as they deliver their bowling balls out over the foul line or as they dump them. Watch to see what action the bowling ball takes after you see a good delivery and a bad delivery. Particularly watch the hand and finger action of good bowlers and see whether or not you can observe the thumb being released ahead of time and the fingers giving the proper, desired finger lift.

I would like to explore with you a little further the timing of the thumb release. Having performed these experiments with the ball being thrown into the chair seat or into the arms of your brave partner, I hope I have convinced you that a proper early "timed" thumb release is absolutely necessary for a good effective bowling delivery.

You must now be aware and agree that the thumb release must occur in time, that is, coordinated with the speed of the body's approach to the line, the physical aspect of the body above it in such a position that the hand, arm, hand, and fingers are all able to get rid of the ball as they must. Still the fingers must have the time, that fraction of a second, for the thumb to get out of the ball and the fingers to stay with it a second or so longer to put the action on it. All of which backs up to the basic proposition of bowling: that the bowler develop a rhythmic, repeating, step-by-step approach timed to the pushaway or dropaway of the ball, all the way through backswing and downswing to the split second of time when the bowler does deliver the ball over the line.

I would like you to consider the picture of a major league baseball pitcher throwing for the strike zone over the plate. If he releases it a second too soon, he has a wild pitch over the catcher's head against the backstop. The timing of the bowling ball release is as critical as that of the baseball pitcher.

Consider also the picture of the golfer making a swing with a driver. He must time his forward and backward swing motion so that his axis of swing remains the same, so that his golf club gets back to the same spot from which it left as it began its backswing. It is my personal conviction that asking a bowler to deliver a timed bowling delivery at a foul line 12 to 16 feet in front of him and to do it time after time successfully in exactly the same manner would be comparable to asking Sam Snead, or any other good golfer, to tee up a ball 12 to 16 feet in front of him and then take four or more steps as he executed the back swing and downswing of the golf club so as to strike the golf ball flush and drive it straight and far down the fairway.

Many good bowlers are also good golfers. I think there is a strong similarity between the two sports. The more I examine both, the more convinced I am that both are very difficult sports to master.

Here is an excellent view of the proper release of the ball. Note that the fingers are still closing, having imparted action to the ball. Note that the ball is still in midair as it travels six inches or so out over the foul line. The thumb hole of the ball has evidently begun to rotate on a 4 o'clock to 10 o'clock axis. The left foot is still in its straight slide to the foul line.

41

Proper release

The moment of truth

THE MOMENT OF TRUTH: THE RELEASE

Here is what I call the moment of truth, the fraction of a second after the fingers have imparted their action to the ball. The fingers have not yet had time to close. The ball is lofted slightly out onto the lane traveling about an inch above the boards for a distance that may vary from about six inches to as much as a foot and a half before it will touch down onto the bowler's line. Note that my sliding foot is heading directly for its designated dot on the approach. Note, too, my concentration on my target out on the lane.

CHAPTER 7

Now, here is some very important advice about your follow-through. One of the most frequent errors bowlers make is what I call a snapping action; they withdraw their fingers from the ball almost as if they can't wait to get rid of it. Other bowlers allow their fingers and hands to lose their firmness at the last second, relaxing their fingers and letting them go limp at the delivery point. You will often see a bowler with a fine smooth approach and good rhythm but note that he is unable to knock down the pins. The reason usually is that he is just not applying the firm fingers in his release.

For you to achieve a good lifting action, one that allows your fingers to impart spin to the ball as it leaves your hand, it is absolutely necessary that your hand, your arm, and your

The Follow-Through

shoulder continue on through the pendulum arm swing at least as long as the ball remains in the hand, until it is pulled from the hand by centrifugal force.

In my opinion, this idea of firmness and of not relaxing the grip, the execution of the follow-through are equally as important as the proper hand and finger action themselves. Remember that no matter how perfect, how rhythmic, how precise your entire bowling swing is through your forward swing, backswing, and downswing to release, if you fail to execute this tensed finger action at the proper moment, your entire bowling act fails.

I do not mind it if you exaggerate your follow through. Try letting your hand and arm come through until your thumb is pointing straight up.

Another good thought which may work for you is this: imagine yourself in the act of bowling and picture yourself having completed a full follow-through. By imprinting your imagination in advance you have that desirable positive thought which may block out another undesirable one, a thought or fear that you might not make the shot that confronts you. Remember that the mind can have only one thought at a time, and your goal is to emphasize the positive thoughts so as to exclude negative ones.

My last word on the follow-through: If you find that you are inconsistent in your ability to accomplish a good follow-through, it is most likely that your timing is incorrect. Your bowling arc is probably not timed to coincide with the proper instant of time so that your ball is at the bottom of the arc as it passes your left, sliding foot.

Too rapid an approach, too slow an approach, a fault in your pushaway, any one of these faults can and does interfere with that moment of truth at the bottom of the bowling swing. The game is not an easy one. It may take years for you to achieve the timing you want and need. Without it you will be an acceptable but erratic bowler. You might even be a bad bowler destined never to raise your average out of the mediocre class. The choice is yours. I am pointing the way for you to successful high scoring bowling and it is up to you to accept the challenge.

Not only must you read and understand the principles and techniques I am teaching you in this book, but you must also plan to get instructions in person from the best teacher of bowling you can find. That teacher may or may not be a member of the Professional Bowlers Association, although if he is, he certainly will be carrying excellent credentials and have worlds of experience. Your instructor may easily be your nearby counter man who has watched you bowl under many differing conditions and knows not only your bowling style and your usual faults but also is knowledgeable about lane conditions.

Study other bowlers' styles, ask questions of the good bowlers—and best of all, practice, practice, practice!

THE FOLLOW-THROUGH

This is an overhead view of my follow-through after a proper delivery. Notice that my arm has come straight up and is heading directly down my intended line, that my sliding knee is bent to allow my body to get down close to the foul line and apply leverage to the shot. Notice, too, that my opposite hand and arm are behind me in their natural movement to counterbalance the weight of the bowling ball. There should be a definite sense of "staying down at the line" until the ball is well on its way to its target.

Follow-through

Here is another view of the follow-through, which is absolutely necessary in order to bowl a ball with action. The thumb is clearly still on the inside and the back of the hand and the wrist are still flat. Squareness to the line is very clear in the hips and, in general, in the attitude of the bowler's entire body.

Squareness to the line in follow-through

Deep knee bend

Here is a demonstration of the deep knee bend that is necessary in order to get down to the foul line and be in a suitable position to deliver the bowling ball an inch or so above the lane surface. The right hand and arm follow through straight down the line the ball is taking. There is no thought nor execution of a turn of the body or shoulder toward the true target, the 1-3 pocket. The bowler must have confidence in the action in the ball to produce the hook at the end of its travel down the lane. Any turning inward toward the head pin amounts to killing the ball, to loss of action. It is one of the most frequent faults of the moderately good bowler who wonders why he never seems to improve to championship caliber.

CHAPTER 8

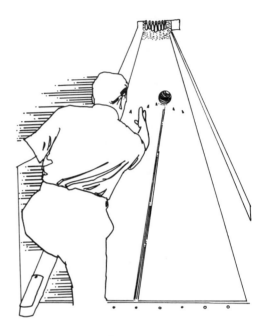

The most important pin in the entire bowling pin setup is the 5-pin. It has been called the kingpin for many years, and truly it is the "King of Strikes." Miss it with your ball or fail to get it with pin action that causes another pin to knock it down and you do not have a strike. In fact, often times you may have a split with the stubborn 5-pin one of its components.

It is most important that you understand the term bowling angle which is sometimes called just angle. By "angle" we mean the angle of direction taken by the bowling ball as it enters the 1-3 pocket on its way, the bowler hopes, to the kingpin, the 5-pin. If you draw an imaginary straight line from the right-hand corner of the lane to the 5-pin in the complete pin setup, you will have at the end of that track what I would call normal angle for a bowling ball to enter the 1-3 pocket. The angle we are

Understanding Angle
and Deflection

discussing refers only to the last three or four feet of that line. So, it follows that if your bowling ball has a large hook at the end of its travel, in order to allow your ball to come into the pocket at the normal line of angle it is necessary for you to deliver the ball somewhere toward the center of the lane so as to let the ball roll just far enough and long enough so that at the end of its travel, the hooking action on your ball will take over and let it enter the pocket at the desired angle toward the 5-pin.

It has been shown by using machines that roll identical bowling balls one after the other that a ball that comes from the outside corner of the lane straight toward the 1-3 pocket and then hooks into the pocket toward the 5-pin will produce strike after strike.

But unfortunately lane conditions have a great deal to do with this situation. Most bowlers deliver their balls on a line some-where near the second arrow on the lane, and the result is that a ball track is worn in the lane from the friction of so many balls traveling the same line. So the bowler who uses outside angle with a ball that comes directly from the corner runs into difficulty when he has to cross that worn track or get into the track as it approaches the pocket.

An understanding of angle must include an understanding of the ball track itself. The bowling ball is 27 inches in circumfer-ence, which means that at its equator, or middle, it is some 9 inches wide. The middle of the bowling pin is 4¾ (4.766) inches wide. So, adding double the width of the bowling ball to the width of the pin, it is evident that a bowling track of 9 inches plus 4¾ inches plus 9 inches—nearly 23 inches—exists to operate in knocking down any particular pin. (Note the later discussion of the difficulty of making 7 and 10 pins as a result of losing some of the track on one side, the right side for the 10-pin, the left side for the 7-pin, and see the photo below.) You should now understand why there is an old bowling adage "You should never miss a 1-pin spare." How can you when you are shooting at a target 23 inches wide?

Now, let's talk about deflection of the bowling ball. I would like to suggest that some day you ask your friendly bowling proprietor to let you go back into the bowling pits and watch bowling ball deflection in action. You will see the bowling ball head for a spare, hit it on one side or the other and then, like lightning, dart to the offside of the spare. That darting is deflection caused by the weight of the bowling pin or pins resisting the weight of the bowling ball and causing it to alter its direction.

The American Bowling Congress has conducted extensive testing to determine whether a 16 pound bowling ball carries more strikes than a 14 pound ball. It concluded that because the 14 pound ball may be able to achieve a greater entry angle than the 16 pound ball, there is equal strike capability with either ball. Therefore, it follows that the average bowler would be better off rolling the lighter, less physically trying ball.

My own preference remains with the 16 pound ball, for I have a psychological need to hit the pins with all the weight and power I can get, but I recommend that you experiment with a lighter ball. Perhaps you will find that it performs as well as or even better than the heavier ball.

During the same tests, Dan Speranza, manager of the Equipment Specifications Department of the American Bowling Congress test facility, also determined the best entry angle for the ball into the 1-3 pocket to cause a strike. "Entry angle" is the angle of the ball into the pins. "Offset" is the number of inches the ball is away from hitting the head-pin straight on. The highest strike percentage occurs at an offset of about $2\frac{1}{2}$ inches (plus or minus $\frac{1}{8}$ inch), which is the location of the ball from the center of the head pin, measured across the lane. The best entry angle for consistent strikes was determined to be 6 degrees. This conclusion may surprise many bowlers who have the impression that the bowling ball needs to enter the 1-3 pocket at a greater angle (10 degrees to 15 degrees, for example).

We cannot argue with technology and high-speed cameras. They give us the definitive answer. Our challenge is to find the ball that suits us best and delivers a consistent 6 degree entry angle into the pins.

So, with this explanation of angle and deflection, let us now proceed to analyze the various splits and spare combinations you will encounter. When you note that I recommend attacking a spare or a split from a certain angle you will be aware that the reason for such an attack is to enable you to take advantage of your ball track and to reduce the chance that deflection will cause you to miss a second or third pin in a set-up. You will be using that 23 inch width of the ball track to its best advantage.

WHY IT IS SO EASY TO LEAVE (BE "TAPPED ON") A 10-PIN, A 7-PIN, OR A 4-PIN

Sometimes it seems that your strike ball gets under the pins and starts them revolving in a horizontal plane so that, like windmills, they catch the other pins that are still standing and knock them down. And then again, sometimes your ball will knock the pins straight across the lane and they touch nothing as they go. Always remember that you have a lovely 15-inch wide track clearing out pins for you if your pins fly crossways but if they go straight through you have only a four inch track. That's why you may often lose a pin or two on what seems to be a good hit.

Right-hander's footwork for extreme inside angle

Don't worry about it, the luck will always even out in the long run!

EXTREME INSIDE ANGLE FOR A RIGHT-HANDER

Although you might think that this is the desired footwork for a left-handed bowler, it is really a set of footprints of the necessary footwork for a right-handed bowler who wishes to bowl the deepest possible inside angle. From this delivery point the right-handed bowler will roll slightly to the right of center lane in the hope of delaying his hit until the ball gets near the pocket. My only advice to you on this shot, is that you should never try it unless you are in desperation and no other angles have worked for you. It is one of the most difficult angles in bowling.

THE SECOND AND THIRD ARROW SHOT

On the next page (top) is a photo showing an arrow that has been added to point to a lane marker that indicates the line over which 90 percent of all righthanded bowlers roll. It may vary a board or two to either side (as shown in the bottom photo), but in general this is the line I recommend that you attempt to use for greatest success. With your left foot on the center dot of the seven dots behind the foul line in the approach area, your shoulder will bring your bowling swing in line with one of these boards between the second and third arrows at the "break of the boards". This is the line I want you to square your self to, the spot I want you to keep your eye on as you deliver your ball. You should train yourself to stay down at the foul line and watch to see whether or not you are hitting your target here between the arrows. Remember that one board to the right or left will result in 14 inches of variation in the place you strike near the pocket.

BOWLING THE THIRD ARROW SHOT
FROM INSIDE ANGLE

This is a demonstration of how to bowl deep inside angle. Notice that the ball has been placed out onto the lanes about ten boards inside the third arrow at the break of the boards, indicated by the arrows. This angle brings about a ball which heads out toward the right and then catches the track and starts to make its own move. It requires a very powerful bowler and powerful ball to accomplish this shot, for the ball has a lot of work to do to get back and carry in the pocket. Notice that the bowler is square to his intended line, not to his eventual target which is the 1-3 pocket, of course. His hips are square, too, and his follow-through goes directly toward his spot at the arrows.

Third arrow inside–angle shot

57

PLAYING THE OUTSIDE LINE

Every bowler will occasionally leave the 5-pin on a 1-3 pocket hit or, worse yet, will leave the 5-7 split or the 8-10 strike split. Of course, for the good bowler or the poorer bowler, these leaves are a sure signal that the ball has deflected to the right as it rolled into the pocket and failed to do its proper work on the 5-pin. Playing the incorrect angle to the pocket and to the 5-pin will encourage these troublesome leaves. Remember that the more your ball must generate its own angle into the 1-3 pocket, the more chance you have of losing power at the very end of the ball's roll and having it subject to deflecton to the right.

So, I recommend that the bowler who does not roll a strong ball, that is, one with good hitting power and an authoritative snap hook at the end of its travel, consider using the outside line to the pocket. The reason is that the less strong ball (I hesitate to say weaker) will deflect less if it enters the 1-3 pocket from the outside of the lane rather than from the inside of the lane.

This outside angle is a necessity for the straight ball bowler and for many women bowlers who bowl with lighter weight bowling balls. It is an excellent line, too, for the male bowler with only a slight hook or one who rolls a lighter bowling ball himself.

PLAYING EXTREME OUTSIDE ANGLE

This is a diagram of a first arrow shot. It can be devastating under certain lane conditions that do not cause the bowler's hook to jump too quickly into the pocket but rather allow it to set and drive straight for the 5-pin. Actually the ball stays out of the customary trough or track until the very last second and then makes its move. It is a good line on very stiff lanes, those that resist taking the hook.

First arrow shot

CHAPTER 9

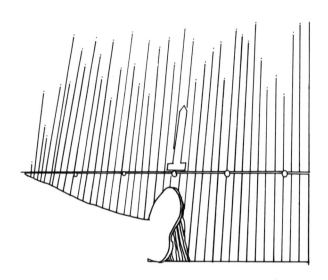

Because of differing lane conditions and because the bowler is sometimes facing ten pins and other times any number from nine to one in varying combinations, you need to know different starting positions.

The most basic starting position is that which you take when you are rolling your first ball with the intention of knocking down all ten pins—a strike.

So the first basic starting position is Strike Position.

STRIKE POSITION

Your starting position for a strike hit will normally be with your left

The Five Basic
Starting Positions

foot on the center dot of the approach (next page) which brings your right shoulder in line with your strike line. For the Left Center Group (see p. 72) with the 5-pin you will also always bowl from your natural strike position primarily because of the presence of the 5-pin. The 5-pin is the kingpin, and it must be gotten out of the cluster. For your second ball with the Left Center Group your strike angle is the best one to use.

Strike Position, Crossover Line

This picture illustrates at the "break of the boards" what I mean by the Strike Position, Crossover Line. Let us presume that the bowler has found that his strike line is down the eighteenth

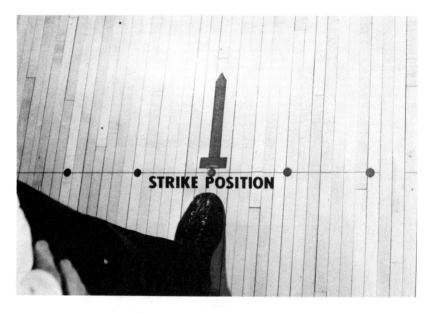

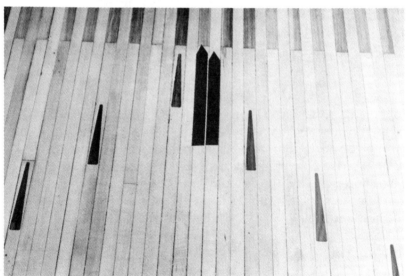

Strike position, crossover line

board, that is, the third board to the left of the third arrow. That line takes his ball into the 1-3, or strike, pocket. By rolling his ball from the same starting positon but one board to the left of that strike line, his ball will cross over and come into the Brooklyn, or 1-2, pocket. This is a most valuable shot to understand and to master because it simplifies the making of many spares which have the 1-2 combination left standing.

LEFT CENTER STARTING POSITION

Place your left foot on the seventh board left of the center dot. Square your body toward the pins and your spare. This shot is slightly cross-alley. You will use this starting position for Right Center Group pins. If your spare should happen to have pins from both the Right Center Group and also from the Far Right Group, the importance of getting the pins in the Center Group determines your starting position and dictates your start from Left Center.

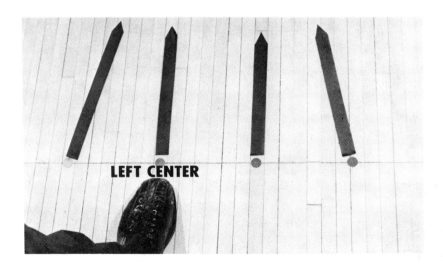

LEFT CENTER

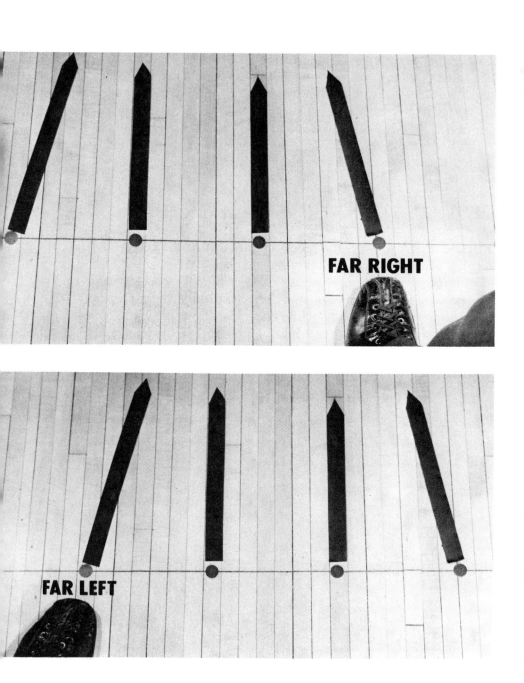

FAR RIGHT STARTING POSITION

This is Far Right Starting Position, which you will use to convert spares on the Far Left side of the lane. You will place your left toe, your target foot, on the seventh board to the right of Strike Position and, squaring your body for your line through your target at the break of the boards, the dart-shaped range finders 12 to 16 feet out on the lane, you will bowl on an angle cross-lane.

FAR LEFT STARTING POSITION

Place your left foot on the 14th board left of the center, or strike, dot. Face directly toward the pins on the far right side of the lane. Your approach will be decidedly cross-alley. You must be aware, however, that since your ball will be delivered from the right-hand side of your body, your actual delivery point from this Left Center Starting Position will be approximately at the center of the lane. Swing your arm directly toward the pins and do not ease up in any manner lest your ball run away on you at the end of its travel. Furthermore, attempt to deliver the ball with your normal speed and action lest you kill it and find it dropping off to the right in the channel (gutter; depressed area on each side of the lane). Use this Far Left Starting Position for Far Right Group spares.

CHAPTER 10

When the good bowler delivers the first ball of each frame he has two objectives in mind. First of all, he wants to get a strike. But if he can't get a strike, he does not want to have a leave, that is, pins standing after the first ball has been delivered that he cannot easily clear with his second ball. If the good bowler does have to bowl a second ball in a frame, he applies just as much concentration to that second shot as he did on his first shot so as to convert the spare if it is at all possible. The poorer bowler tries hard to make his strike on his first ball but oftentimes can be seen to give up when it comes to his second shot and trying to make the spare. The difference between the poor and the good bowler in this regard can amount to from 20 to as much as 40 pins in an average over an entire season.

The Spares and How to Make Them

Most leaves can be converted into spares if you will concentrate on them, understand them in the sense that you bowl for them from the best possible angle so as to take advantage of the ball track and the ball action. It is also true that the same careful attention to many splits not including the headpin (leaves of two or more pins with intervening space left where pins have fallen) will bring results in conversions of them as well.

The secret in shooting spares and in converting splits is in knowing and understanding what each pin is supposed to do once the chain reaction of ball into pocket has been accomplished. I am using the word "pocket" loosely here. In the 2-4-5-spare combination, the pocket is the 2-5, for example. Once you know the secret your object is to guide your ball to the spot that will start the chain reaction to get you the help you need from the other pin or pins to make the conversion. I hope that I can reveal to you in the following pages the secrets of successful spare and split conversions.

THE BASIC PIN GROUPS FOR MAKING SPARES

You should memorize this diagram of the various groups for making spares, for they control your starting position for the conversion of spares and many of the splits. The 4-7-8 make up the Far Left Group, the 6-9-10 the Far Right Group. If you reverse the name of the group, in general, you have your starting position. Far Left = Far Right Starting Position, for example. In the center of the lane is the Left Center Group which has the 1-2-5-8 pins and the Right Center Group with the 1-3-5-9 pins. You will learn in a moment how the presence or absence of the 5-pin makes quite a difference in your starting position for converting the Center Groups. Left Center Group spares, in general, are bowled from Right Center Starting Position, which is usually Strike Position as well. Right Center Group spares are bowled from Left Center Starting Position.

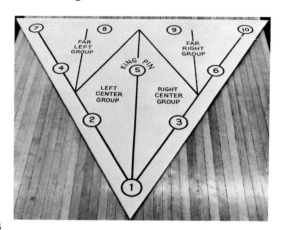

Basic pin groups

The Far Left Group

The 4-, 7-, and 8-pins constitute the Far Left Group. Without exception, they should be bowled from Far Right Starting Position. Always remember to allow for the extra distance the ball must travel to get to the back row of pins and for that reason choose a line or spot slightly to the right of the line your eye tells you to use. You will find that you will miss this spare most often on the left-hand side because of your failure to make this suggested allowance.

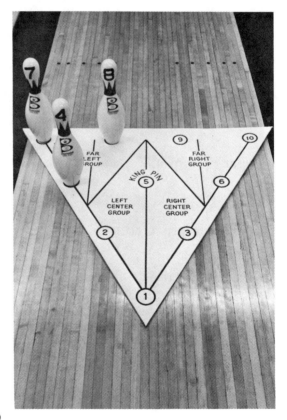

Far left group

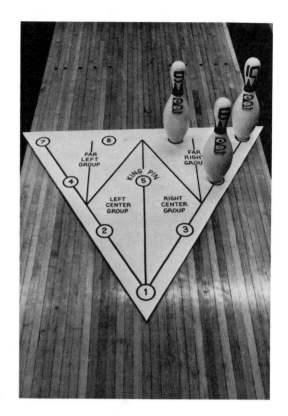

Far right group

The Far Right Group

The 6-, 9-, and 10-pins are in the Far Right Group. You should always bowl for them from Far Left Starting Position.

The only exception is that you may find that you are able to convert the 9-pin alone from Left Center Position because it is also a part of that group. But if you have the 6-pin standing with either the 9-pin or the 10-pin, you have better angle, and therefore a better chance to convert, by rolling from Far Left Starting Position.

The Left Center Group (Without the 5-pin)

The 1-, 2-, and 8-pins constitute the Left Center Group (without the 5-pin). You should bowl this spare from your Strike Position, Crossover Line.

By that I mean that you will plan to start in your normal strike position with your left toe on the center spot but you will pick out a board one board to the left of your strike line at the arrows on the lane. By bowling that one board to the left of your normal strike line your ball will travel just enough to the left to hit the 1-2 pocket and go on through to take out the 8-pin immediately afterward. The addition of the 4-pin or 7-pin to this setup does not make any difference. Bowl it from Strike Position, Crossover Line and you will make it nearly every time.

Left center group without 5–pin

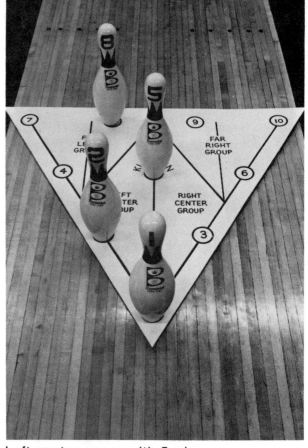

Left center group with 5–pin

The Left Center Group (With the 5-pin)

The 1-, 2-, 5-, and 8-pins make up the Left Center group and because of the presence of the 5-pin you treat this spare just as you would treat a strike setup.

Bowl from your normal strike line right into the 1-3 pocket as if the 3-pin was there. The 5-pin is the controlling factor here; and just as you must get the 5-pin out of a strike setup, you must be certain to put action on your ball so that the ball has enough power to take out the 5-pin. Even if you should happen to have a 4-pin or a 7-pin added to this setup, you should still bowl for it from your strike position down the regular strike line.

HOW TO MAKE THE RIGHT CENTER SPARES

The Right Center Group

The 1-, 3-, 5-, and 9-pins constitute the Right Center Group, and you will use Left Center Starting Position to convert these pins or nearly any combination of them.

If you happen to have the 6-pin or the 10-pin as well, your best strategy is to remain in Left Center Starting Position in order to decrease your chances of cutting off, that is, leaving, one or more of the pins. If the 5-pin is present, you may have to experiment to determine for yourself whether you find it easier to convert this leave from Strike Position or from Left Center. Once you have made that determination, stick with it.

Right center group

73

The 1-3-6-10 Spare, Right Center Group

For this spare, your starting position is the Far Left Starting Position.

This is a wicked spare, one that is often missed even when it is apparently covered. Anytime you must count on pin action (motion of struck pins) to take out part of a spare, you run a chance of missing it. The strategy here is to put your ball into the 1-3 pocket and then get some help from the 6-pin in taking out the 10-pin. If you move too far left for your start, you may end up with the ball sliding by the headpin and, of course, missing the spare. If you move too far right, you may just plain chop right through and leave the 10-pin standing as the 6-pin wraps itself around the 10. Sometimes this spare can be made by hitting the headpin on its left side and counting on pin action to take out the other pins down the line. Your best bet is to try for the pocket and get as many pins as you can with your ball and ball track. Don't be upset at missing this spare. Everyone misses it some time.

The 1-3-6-10 spare

74

The 5-9 Spare, Right Center Group

For the 5-9 spare your starting position is Left Center.

This leave will occur when you have a crossover hit on the Brooklyn side of the pin setup. It is a difficult spare because of your chances of picking off either pin and leaving the other. By bowling from Left Center you have the best angle at this spare. Be certain that you roll your ball a little harder than usual because the pins are farther back than usual, and your ball may take off at the end and chop the 5-pin, leaving the 9-pin. You will have to experiment with this spare to find your own best method of making it. Moving your start a board or two to the right or left may make a big difference in your ability to convert it regularly. Everyone chops this (hits the front pin and leaves the other) once in a while; so don't get upset if you do, too!

The 5-9 spare

The 1-3-5-9 spare

The 1-3-5-9 Spare, Right Center Group

For the 1-3-5-9 spare, your starting position is Left Center.

This leave will happen frequently on a Brooklyn or crossover hit into the 1-2 pocket where the ball really takes off to the left of the headpin. It is another one of those very difficult spares because of the chance that you may leave one or more of the pins no matter which way you attack the spare. By bowling from Left Center you will have the best angle to make this spare. But don't get too far left, or your ball will not have enough action on it to get the 5-pin or possibly the 9-pin after it has gotten the 5-pin. You may even try to make this spare from your normal strike position, treating it as a baby strike. It is a tough one. Don't be too upset when you miss it. Even the best bowlers do sometimes!

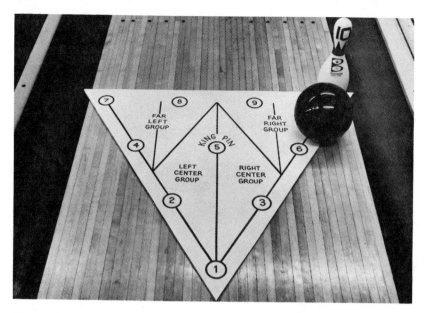

The 10–pin spare

HOW TO MAKE THE FAR RIGHT SPARES

The 10-pin Spare, Far Right Group

For the 10-pin spare, your starting position is Far Left.

This spare is one of the most frequently missed "easy" spares in bowling. The 7-pin is equally as difficult for the left-hander. Since the 10-pin is in the back row of pins, your ball has a tendency to take off in its hooking action at the end, thus causing you to miss this pin on the left. On the other hand, if you speed up your ball you may lose some of your action and find that your ball falls into the channel short of making the pin. I recommend practice on making this 10-pin in these various ways: imagine a pin standing in the channel and shooting for it, or find your own spot at the arrows which will usually take your ball through the 10-pin. Whatever you do, don't loaf on the shot. Also, be sure you follow through because the least pull to the left will cause a miss. Always try to hit the 10-pin flush, and then you will have some margin of error if your ball acts erratically at the end of its track.

Why It Is So Easy To Miss the 10-pin

Look closely at the picture above, and you will see that because there are only two and one-half inches between the 10-pin and the right-hand channel, you do not have the advantage of the width of your entire ball track on the right side of the lane. The same thing holds true, in reverse, for the 7-pin on the left side. Thus your target on these two pins is about seven inches narrower than it would normally be for a single pin spare standing in the center of the lane. Be certain to use cross-lane angle on either one of these spares and even more caution than usual to make sure you hit them in dead center. The least variation on either side toward the channel will cost you the spare.

My Way to Convert the 10-pin, the 6-10, the 3-6-10 and the 3-10 Split

Probably the toughest spare for a beginner to convert is the 10-pin. It is one of the toughest for the professional bowlers, too. You will often see the 10-pin missed in televised matches when the pressure is the greatest and the bowler "quits" in his delivery and allows the ball to run into the channel long before it hits the 10-pin target, or else the bowler will pull his shot as he delivers it and the ball misses the target on the left.

Some bowlers insist on using their normal hook when they are trying for the 10-pin; the 6-10, the 3-6-10, and the 2-10 split. Others go so far as to throw a backup ball at them, that is, a ball that goes to the right, the opposite of a hook. My style is somewhat a compromise between these two balls. Of course, we all start our approach from the extreme left side of the lane in order to give as much angle as possible for the pesky 10-pin standing on the far right side of the pin deck.

What I do is "flatten" my ball, that is, I keep it rolling straight so that there is neither a hook nor a backup action. I do this by altering the position of my thumb in my backswing. The thumb is twisted around in a clockwise fashion so that it is at 2 o'clock and the palm of my hand is facing outward from my body. Then as I bring my arm and hand down and through in the release I make sure that I keep the thumb in the same 2 o'clock position. The result is that the ball goes off my hand with an end-over-end roll straight down the lane. I get no hook on this type of release, and if I aim it properly the ball does not vary in its straight path toward the 10-pin.

I do the same thing with the 3-6-10, the 3-10, and 6-10 spares. With this difference, I shoot at the right-hand side of the head-pin of each setup and aim straight at my target. Of course, the headpin of these leaves would be the 3-pin in the 3-6-10, the 6-pin in the 6-10 and the 3-pin in the 3-10. I feel that a hook ball is too apt to pick off the 3-pin from the 3-6-10 or 3-10 leave or the 6-pin from the 6-10 leave. There is another factor at work here, too, and that is that when you roll the straight ball rather than the hook, your ball will deflect more to the right as it hits the front 3-pin of the 3-6-10 spare, the 6-pin of the 6-10 spare, or the 3-pin of the 3-10 split. In these instances you want this deflection. It helps to send the ball more to the right so as to touch and thus convert the right-hand pins which remain standing once the headpin of the the setup is toppled.

I seem to make more of those mean spares my straight ball way. You should give my method a try. It might work for you, too.

The 6-10 Spare, Far Right Group

For the 6-10 spare, your starting position is Far Left.

Along with its counterparts, the 5-9 and the 2-5, this spare is a difficult one for the right-handed bowler because of the tendency of the curving ball to cut sharply through the front pin and take it off the other pin which remains, a "cherry," as bowlers call a pin left standing when a pin in front is chopped. I suggest that you bowl to make the 10-pin full because you will find that nearly always your ball will move slightly at the end of its track and get the 6-pin for you. This spare is great for 6-7-10 split practice, too. You will be able to tell whether you would have driven the 6-pin across the lane to take out the imaginary 7-pin.

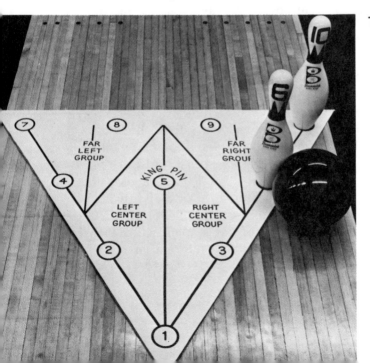

The 6-10 spare

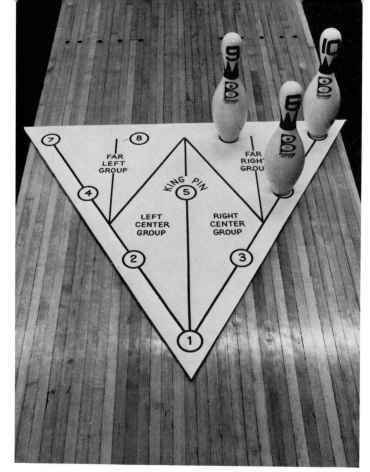

The 6–9–10 spare

The 6-9-10 Spare, Far Right Group

For the 6-9-10 spare, your starting position is Far Left.

Imagine that this leave is a baby strike; so plan to hit it in its right-hand pocket. Don't think about the 9-pin because you will probably get it with the 6-pin while the ball goes on to take out the 10-pin. The reason you should always try to make this on its right-hand side is that if you do make a mistake in your delivery and pull it or if your ball runs away at the end as it sometimes does as it gets on into the pin deck, you still have a chance to make the spare in its left-hand pocket, or as bowlers say, on the outside. This is an easy spare to miss. Be careful with it!

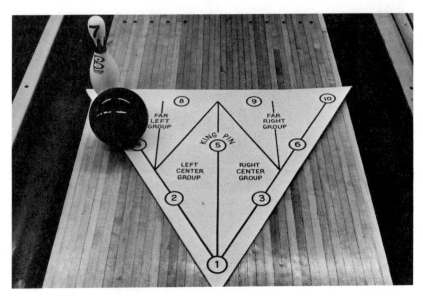

The 7-pin spare

HOW TO MAKE THE FAR LEFT SPARES

The 7-pin Spare, Far Left Group

For the 7-pin spare, your starting position is Far Right.

Because this pin is so close to the channel, remember that your target is cut down by about seven inches. Because your ball will be curving into the pin rather than away as it does on the 10-pin spare, however, this spare is easier to convert than the 10-pin spare, at least for the right-hander. The opposite is true for the left-hander, of course. Be sure that you don't ease up on this spare, or your ball may run away to the left and cause you to miss it. Line yourself up squarely for a shot at the right-hand side of the pin because that is where your greatest margin of error lies. Go after it with authority. You should make this spare every time.

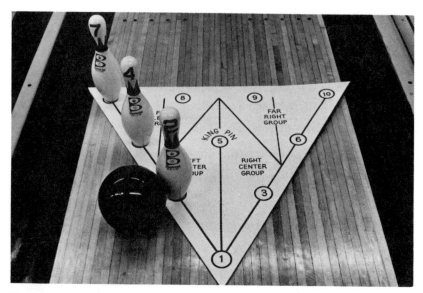

The 2–4–7 spare

The 2-4-7 Spare, Far Left Group

For the 2-4-7 spare, your starting position is Far Right.

Plan to hit the 2-pin on its left side and let the ball deflect into the 4-pin and continue on its way to the 7-pin. Even if the ball does not get all the way to the 7-pin, the 4-pin may help you by deflecting into the 7-pin for you and taking it out. You must take advantage of the cross-alley angle on this spare because if the ball comes in from the left on the 4-pin you may hit it too far on its right side and it may "wrap around" the 7-pin and miss it. Sometimes you may see this spare made by hitting the 2-pin on its right side and letting the 4-pin go on to take out the 7-pin. I do not recommend this because there is too much of a chance that the 7-pin may be left.

HOW TO MAKE THE LEFT CENTER SPARES

The 2-4-5-8 Spare, Left Center Group

For the 2-4-5-8 spare, your starting position is Left Center.

This spare is one of the most dreaded that any bowler will encounter. Even when it is struck with an ideal spare ball, it seems that sometimes a pin will be chopped. I recommend treating this setup as a baby strike and moving to your left for your starting position. Bowl it straightaway, that is, as if it were a strike setup and plan to have your ball come into the 2-5 pocket the same way you would normally come into the 1-3 pocket if it were a strike. Your ball must be rolled with action so that it carries on through to take out the 8-pin. If you get too high on the 2-pin your ball may fail to take out the 5-pin. Once in a while you

The 2-4-5-8 spare

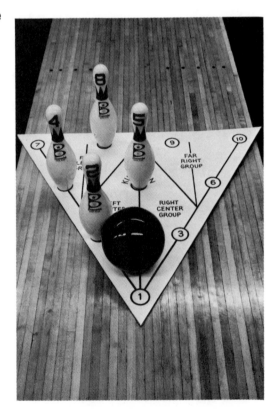

may get lucky when you really have missed this spare and still convert it by bouncing a pin off the side wall (the kickback on each side of the pin deck) to take out a pin that would otherwise have been a cherry.

The Left Center Group (with the 5 Pin)

For the 1-2-5-8 spare your start position is Strike Positon.

This cluster might just as well be the entire setup of ten pins. The presence of the 5-pin is crucial here because just as it is the kingpin in the strike setup, it is the kingpin here, too. You must roll a ball with action to get this center group in order to power through and get the 5-pin. Even if you have the 4-pin or the 7-pin added to this spare you will still attack it from the Strike Position.

The left center group

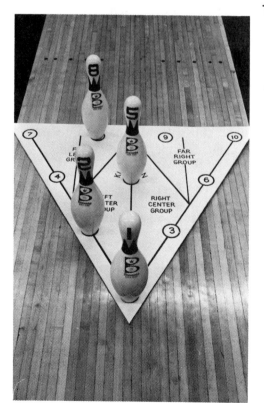

85

SHOOTING THE 2-4-5, THE 2-4-5-8 "BUCKET," OR JUST THE 2-4 OR 2-8 SPARES

When I shoot at these spares, I roll from the left side of the lane in contrast to the way I normally shoot at left-hand side spares from the right-hand side, or "cross the lane" as it is called.

I believe that, at least for me, I cut down the chances of picking off pins in any one of these groups. I'm rolling in a slick part of the lane, out of the normal track, usually where there is not as much ball traffic or track as there is on the right side of the lane. There will be more oil remaining on the left-hand side of the lane so that my ball is not apt to break as much as it would if it were on the usual track. All these conditions mean that I must slow my ball down somewhat and make sure I get some hook action on my ball as I hit the 2-5 pocket just as if I were aiming for the 1-3 pocket on a first ball. ˙

I find that this method works for me. It may work for you, too. You should try both "crossing the lane" at them and then my method of moving left on them. Try one method for a good length of time and keep track of your misses and chops. Then try the other style and compare your conversion average. I do recommend, however, that once you decide on the proper method for you of converting these troublesome spares that you stick with that method all the time. You will merely confuse yourself if you change from game to game and method to method.

The 2-4-5 Spare, Left Center Group

For the 2-4-5 spares, your starting position is Strike Position, Crossover Line.

This leave will happen when your first ball is light in the pocket and never reaches the 5-pin. Because there are three pins, it is another one of those troublesome spares. It is easy to pick either the 4-pin or the 5-pin, depending on which way your ball hits the 2-pin on either its right- or left-hand side. Your best bet to convert this spare is to take the crossover line from your normal strike starting position and let the ball come into the 2-5 pocket as if it were coming into a full pin setup for the 1-3 pocket. This strategy is good, too, in case you miss the spare on the left-hand side because your ball may yet cause the 2-pin to go to the right and get the 5-pin. If you keep leaving this spare frequently, it is an indication that you do not have enough action on your ball. You need more finger lift or more angle from the right to get the ball into the pocket.

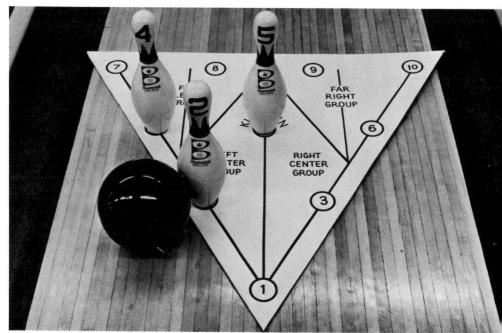

The 2-4-5 spare

The 2-8 Spare, Left Center Group

For the 2-8 spare, your starting positon is Strike Position, Crossover Line.

Bowl this one from your familiar strike starting position, but take the crossover line, which will cause your ball to travel through the 2-pin to take out the 8-pin. This spare is a very demanding one, and the slightest variation to the right or left will result in "picking the cherry," leaving the 8-pin, and thus missing the spare. The 8-pin is often called "your mother-in-law" for obvious reasons. This is a hateful spare because your ball must have enough power to overcome its tendency to deflect away from the 8-pin and thus miss it. Remember that the 2-pin is the same 22 inches in front of the 8-pin that the headpin is in front of the 5-pin. Really concentrate on this spare and any others which have "sleepers," pins hidden behind another.

The 2-8 spare

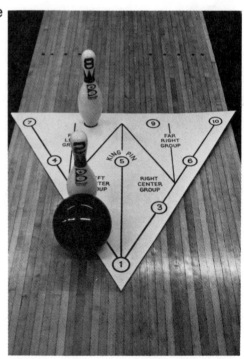

The 1-2-8 Spare, Left Center Group

For the 1-2-8 spare, your starting position is Strike Position, Crossover line.

This spare and other spares related to it like the 1-2-4-8, the 1-2-4-7 and the very unpleasant washout spare, the 1-2-10, are all bowled in exactly the same way, from Strike Position but over the crossover spot at the arrows. I believe that most bowlers feel more comfortable when they bowl in their usual starting position, the strike position; so you should be very relaxed about this spare. Roll your normal strike ball at it, giving your ball normal action and finger lift, to make sure that you carry through to get the 8-pin. If you keep missing the 8-pin on the right-hand side on this spare, it is a sign that you need either more finger lift or more angle. On the other hand, if you keep missing it on the left, it is a sign that you should cut down on your angle by moving left at the start of your approach.

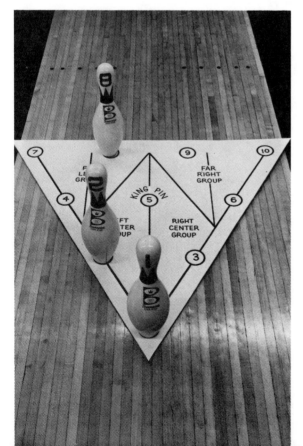

The 1-2-8 spare

The 1-2-10 Washout Spare

For the 1-2-10 Washout Spare, your starting position is Strike Position, Crossover line.

You should be able to convert this spare without too much difficulty. Basically, it is the 1-2 spare which you make comfortably by rolling from your strike position but over the crossover line, which takes your ball into the 1-2 pocket. The 2-pin, having been struck on its left side, is driven over across the lane to take out the 10-pin. This is a flashy spare to make and a very satisfying one. If you leave it very often, it is a sure sign that your ball is not getting to the pocket quickly enough. You may be lofting the ball out onto the lane too far and your action may be starting so late that the ball gets in behind the headpin. You may also be rolling too fast a ball, thus cutting down on the ball action at the pocket. Be sure to roll your normal strike ball on your second effort. The crossover line should work to help you get the 10-pin regularly.

The 1-2-10 spare

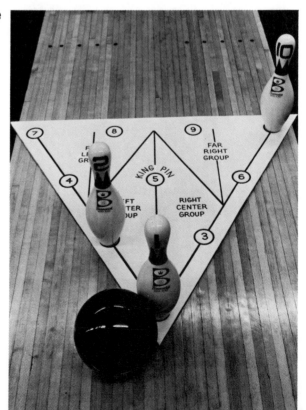

90

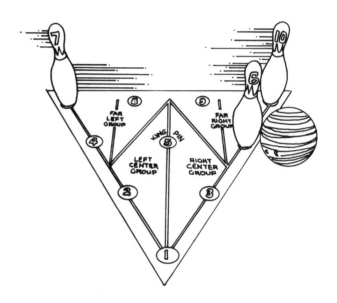

Most splits are the result of some error committed by the bowler, most frequently lack of action on the ball or insufficient angle in the bowling line to the pocket. There are times, however, when the pin-setting equipment may be at fault, and improper mechanical setting of the 5-pin or the 2-pin, or for that matter any other pin, may cause splits. Sometimes it happens that a certain lane has what bowlers call "high spot," an expression to describe a lane condition just short of the pocket which causes the ball to skid and deflect from its normal digging action and cause a split to occur.

Do not hesitate to request a re-rack of your bowling pin setup if you notice any irregularity about the pins. If you think the pocket is unusually open with a bad pin setting you may have

The Splits and How
to Make Them

your confidence undermined and you may not roll your normal
delivery. If after you have gotten a re-rack, you continue to believe that the rack is bad, tell the lane operator about the problem. He will be anxious to check into the accuracy of the pin-
setting equipment and make certain that the pins are being set in
a proper fashion.

Years ago when pins were set by hand it was common knowledge that the human pin-setters could be bribed to set the 5-pin
an inch or so out of its proper position and that an 8-10 split
would often result on an apparently good hit. On the other
hand, when the bribe-taker wanted his benefactor to get a strike,
he would move the 5-pin close to the pocket and chances were
better then for a strike. Many a match in head-to-head competi-

tion was won or lost through the help or hindrance of the human pin-setter. We are fortunate now to have automatic pin-setting machines. They are difficult to bribe!

The 2-7 split

HOW TO MAKE THE FIT-IT-IN-BETWEEN SPLITS

The 2-7 Fit-It-In-Between Split, also known as the Left-Hand Baby Split

Your starting position is Far Right.

Although this split can be made from the outside, meaning that you strike the 2-pin on its right side and throw it into the 7-pin, I recommend that you convert it by striking the 2-pin on the left side and then letting the ball continue in its track to take out the 7-pin. It is easier for the right-handed bowler to make this baby split than it is for him to make the right-hand baby split, the 3-10, because his ball is curving into the 7-pin rather than away from the 10-pin as it is in the 3-10 conversion. If it helps you to convert this split by imagining the missing 4-pin in the set-up, by all means do so. You should practice making this split and the similar 3-10 so that you convert them regularly.

The 3-10 Fit-It-In-Between Split

Your starting position is Far Left.

This split is known as the right-hand baby split. Its counterpart for the left-hander is the 2-7. It commonly occurs on a crossover hit into the 1-2 pocket and is a sign of an inaccurate first ball. There are several strategies you may consider using to convert this split. First, aim at the 10-pin alone and count on some movement left at the end of the ball track to catch the 3-pin. Second, aim to hit the "ghost pins," the missing 6-pin, flush and thus catch both the 3-pin and the 10-pin along the way. Or you may aim to hit the 3-pin thinly on its right side and count on deflection of the ball to take out the 10-pin. Any way you attack it, it is a difficult split, especially for the bowler with a strong ball.

The 3–10 split

The 4-5 Fit-It-In-Between Split

Your starting position is Strike position, Crossover line.

The strike position, crossover line, which takes your ball through the 1-2 pocket, will also enable you to convert this split with regularity. Sometimes it is useful to pretend that you have left only the 5-pin, that the 4-pin has fallen. Just roll the crossover line, hit the 5-pin thinly on its left side and "accidentally" make the 4-pin as well. If you keep getting the 4-pin and missing the 5-pin, try rolling with a little more speed to delay your action at the pocket.

The 5-6 Fit-It-In-Between Split

Your starting position is Left Center. Though bowling from left center, remember to allow a little more to the right than your eye tells you because these pins are in the third row and your ball will be taking off in its curve in the last foot or so of its travel. This is a more difficult split to make than the 4-5 because you will have moved from your familiar strike position and also because your ball will be traveling on a line not frequently used and therefore of unknown characteristics.

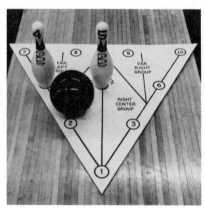

The 4-5 split

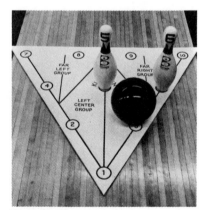

The 5-6 split

96

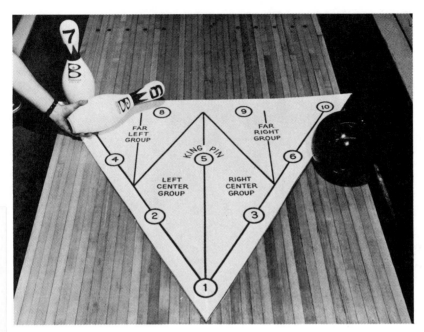

The slide-it-over split

How to Make the Slide-It-Over Splits

As you can see from the illustration above and from analyzing the photographs of many of the wide open splits that follow, if one of the pins is in the row in front of the other pin, or other pins, even if the split is one that is wide open, it is entirely possible for you to convert the split. You accomplish this by striking the pin in the front line thinly, that is, by just barely touching it with your ball, and forcing it to fly across the lane at an oblique angle and thus take out the remaining pin or pins. You should practice a great deal on making the 10-pin "dead on," that is, right in the middle, because it is the same roll of the ball that later on will take out a 6-pin thinly from a 6-7-10 split leave and throw the 6-pin across the lane to get the 7-pin, thus converting the split. Making one of the wide open splits is one of the greatest thrills of bowling. You can do it if you try!

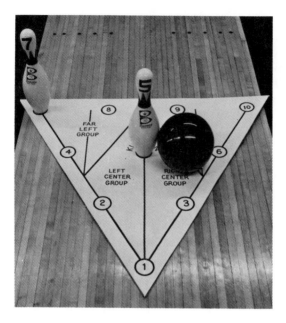

The 5-7 split

The 5-7 Slide-It-Over Split

Your starting position is the Strike Position.

There is a trick to making this split, and once you learn it you should be able to make it with regularity. If you will remember my discussion of the Strike Position, Crossover line, you learned that by bowling from your customary starting position but over a spot one board left of your strike line, your ball would come into the 1-2 pocket for a crossover hit. The trick on this split is that instead of moving your line left at the arrows, you move it right one board and stay in your normal strike starting position. This move causes your ball to go out farther to the right and come into the pocket light so that it will strike the 5-pin thinly and force it over to take out the 7-pin. You must remember to throw your normal strike ball with regular action, that is, don't ease up on the shot. It may be true, too, that you will have to adjust your spot a little more to the right at the arrows, but basically, this is the way to convert the 5-7 spare.

The 5-10

The 5-10 Slide-It-Over Split

Your starting position is Strike Position, Crossover Line.

This split along with the 8-10 split is a sure indicator of a weak ball, one that has failed to get in to the 5-pin, one that has "died in the pocket." If you are getting this split or the 8-10 frequently, you are not getting the proper finger action on your ball. It is also possible that you should have an expert balldriller check the balance of your ball. You might need a stronger ball, one with more finger weight or side weight. You can convert this split by striking the 5-pin thinly on its left side and forcing it across the lane into the 10-pin. I recommend that you try to make it from your normal strike starting position with the ball taking the crossover line, which will bring it into the 5-pin light. If you have trouble making this split from this position, try moving left a board or two from your normal strike position. You would then move your line at the arrows slightly left, too. You will have to experiment until you find the best way for yourself. Once you find it, stay with it. It is a very satisfying split to make.

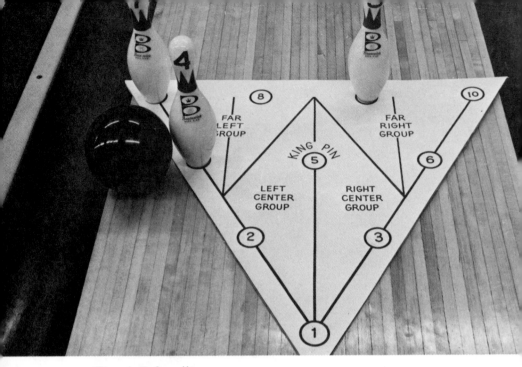

The 4-7-9 split

The 4-7-9 Slide-It-Over Split

Your starting position is Far Right.

This split is bowled, and converted, in much the same way as is the 4-7-10 split. The difference, of course, is that the ball does not have to strike the 4-pin so thinly as it does in order to get the 10-pin in the other split. This split is a warning to the bowler that his ball is coming in too high on the headpin. So if you find that you are getting this leave often, change your angle so that your ball comes into the 1-3 pocket more toward the 3-pin. This split is easier to make than the 4-7-10 because the 9-pin is a foot closer than the 10-pin, and so the 4-pin does not have to travel so far in order to take it out. You might have some success in making this split by pretending that the 9-pin is not even there and by bowling for a thin conversion of the 4-7. You can make this split if you practice hard on it. But, again, be aware of possible loss of count if you do not make the 4-pin at all in you effort to hit it thinly.

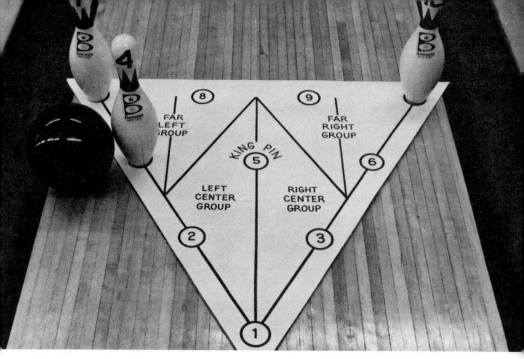

The 4–7–10 split

The 4-7-10 Slide-It-Over Split

Your starting position is Far Right.

Your strategy on this split is to strike the 4-pin thinly on its left side so as to slide it over across the lane and thus take out the 10-pin. It is a very delicate shot and if the 4-pin is hit at all full, you just won't achieve enough angle to have it get the 10-pin. This split is considerably harder to convert than its opposite, the 6-7-10, because your ball will be running away from the 4-pin while it is running into the 6-pin in the other setup and helping it to get across the lane to do its work on the 7-pin. My own personal strategy on this split is to aim for the 7-pin and forget about making the split. Oftentimes, it happens that the hit on the 7-pin is so full that the 4-pin is clipped lightly on its left-hand side and forced across the lane for the conversion of the 10-pin. I recommend that you try to convert this split only when loss of pin count won't hurt your team or your own individual match game. Most of the time it is best to get the two pins for sure and take advantage of the count.

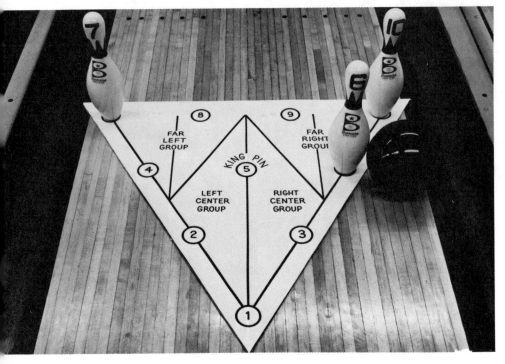

The 6–7–10 split

The 6-7-10 Slide-It-Over Split

Your starting position is Far Left.

Aim for the 10-pin and attempt to hit it on its right side, even if you miss the 6-pin. The result will be that your ball will be snapping in strongly on the right-hand side of the 6-pin, and it will be tossed over sharply across the lane to take out the 7-pin. Be certain that you use good speed on this shot, for the least bit of slowing down will spoil the shot as the ball may break too strongly into the 6-pin and cost you the conversion. Another point is that it takes good speed to impart enough power to the 6-pin in order to drive it across the lane. It is most discouraging to hit it with so little power that it travels part way across the lane and then fails to get the other pin.

THE "IMPOSSIBLE" SPLITS

The 8-10 "Impossible" Split

Your starting position is Strike Position, Crossover Line.

This split usually occurs when your ball dies, or flattens on a 1-3 pocket hit. It is a nasty split and a discouraging one because you have had hopes that you might get a strike. This split will pop up when your ball lacks proper roll. Possibly you overturned your ball, causing too much spin and not enough roll. Another reason might be that you did not use enough angle to the pocket and the ball deflected. Don't lose the opportunity to practice on the 10-pin, that is, if you are bowling in practice. You might even practice on the 3-10 split by imagining the 3-pin in front of the 10. If you are in competition, get your easiest pin for count.

The 8-10 split

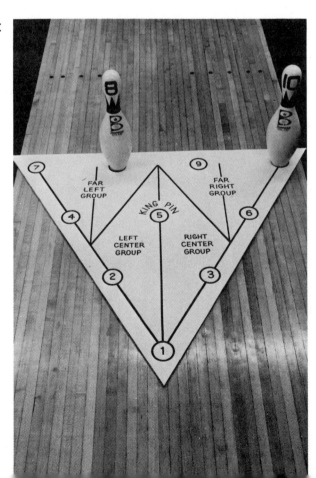

The 4-6-7-10 "Impossible" Split

This famous split, called Double Pinochle, is one of the most dreaded splits in bowling. It will happen when your ball goes in directly on the nose of the pin setup and usually without action. Be aware of loss of count if you do not convert at least two of these pins, so work on this split and get either the 4-7 or the 6-10. You can use this split to practice making the 4-7-10 split or the opposite 6-7-10 split. Once in a great while you may see the 7-pin or the 10-pin fall forward and come off the kickback (the side wall on each side of the pin deck) to take out the front remaining pin and actually convert this very difficult, if not impossible split. There is great rejoicing when this happens, and the occurrence is so rare that the American Bowling Congress will award you a shoulder patch if you do make it.

The 4-6-7-9-10 "Impossible" Split

Although this leave is rare, it does happen sometimes when you might expect to have Double Pinochle alone. Oddly enough, it is more makable, if any "impossible" split can be called makable, than the 4-6-7-10 because if you approach this split as if you were trying to make the 4-7-9 split, which we know is a Slide-it-over and therefore makable split, you may be able to throw the 9-pin into the left-hand side of the 10-pin and with luck have the 10-pin come off the wall and take out the 6-pin. I have seen this happen several times in my career, and it is a sensational happening when it occurs. So make the 4-7-9 split out of this ugly cluster and hope for the best!

The 4–6–7–10 split

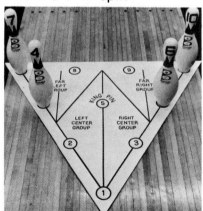

The 4–6–7–9–10 split

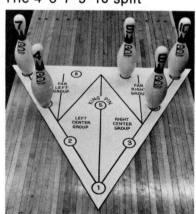

The 4-6 "Impossible" Split

This split, like the 4-6-7-10, will occur when your ball comes in too high on the headpin. In team bowling or other competition, work on your easiest pin and make it to add to your count. If you are practicing, bowl at the pin you usually find hardest to convert. Practice hitting the 4-pin or the 6-pin dead on or on its left or right side as you determine, remembering that your skill at hitting either the 4 or 6 where you want it will add to your ability to convert the 4-7-10 split or the 6-7-10 split. You can even bowl at an imaginary 4-7-10 split or imaginary 6-7-10, and by watching what happens when you hit the 4-pin or the 6-pin, you can tell whether you would have made the split. If you do make it in your imagination, it is almost as much fun as it is in reality, and you will take the sting out of having had a split in the first place.

The 7-9 "Impossible" Split

Whenever you get a so-called "impossible split," take advantage of the opportunity to practice on it. If you have been having trouble with the 7-pin, work on that pin. Experiment with your starting position by moving a board to the right or left from your normal Far Right starting position. You might try the same experiment on the 9-pin. Aim to hit either pin absolutely flush. That kind of practice will help your ability to make some of the more makable splits when a pin must be hit precisely in order to force it to take out another pin. In league play don't experiment. Get your easiest pin and the greatest count possible.

The 4–6 split

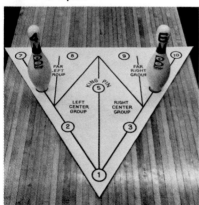

The 7–9 split

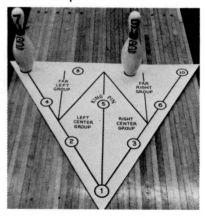

CHAPTER 12

HOW TO ADD MORE EASILY BY SUBTRACTING

Bowling is scored on a sheet by markings which are very distinctive. For each of the ten frames in each game, the score sheet has a box for each frame with a little square in its upper right corner, like this:

The upper right-hand square is used to indicate whether or not the bowler:

1. Knocked all ten pins down with his first ball for a strike, which would be scored:

How to Score in Bowling

2. Knocked all ten pins down with two balls for a spare, which would be scored:

3. Or did not knock down all ten pins with one or two balls, thus scoring a miss, or open frame, officially called an error, which would be scored:

And, as if to take the sting out of an open frame which is the result of a split, the early bowlers devised a symbol to show that the bowler really couldn't help not knocking them all down in two tries because they were too far apart. The scoring mark for an open frame from a split is:

Once in a while when a bowler makes a split or knocks down the separated pins with his second ball, the split mark is crossed through with the spare mark, and the bowler rejoices at filling what appeared to be an open frame with a

Another interesting mark you will run across is a letter c, which is sometimes used to indicate a missed spare where there were originally two pins close together, such as in the 6-10 spare, and the bowler in attempting to make the spare chops off one or the other of the two pins.

Sometimes when you are watching a bowling match, either individual or team, you will see the scorekeeper keeping a numbered tally between the scoring lines and, frame by frame, it may look something like this:

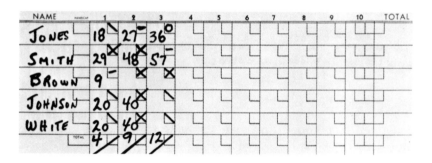

The score sheet indicates the total number of strikes and spares, cumulatively from the first frame through the ninth. Each spare or strike of a team member counts one mark, or approximately ten pins. By totaling marks frame by frame the overall scoring position can be determined fairly accurately.

When one team is spotted a certain number of pins as a handicap, the marks are usually added in either the first frame or else at random throughout the game, as if a phantom bowler were coming up with crucial marks when the team most needed them.

NAME	HANDICAP	1	2	3	4	5	6	7	8	9	10	TOTAL
JONES		18	27	36								
SMITH		29	48	57								
BROWN		9	X	X								
JOHNSON		20	40									
WHITE		20	40									
TOTAL		4	9	12								

Once in a while you'll hear the expression, "take a mark off," by which you'll know a bowler has just had a very bad count, four pins or fewer on a spare or strike, and thus has cost his team ten pins. And, as a matter of interest, you'll always hear the remark from the opponents' team, not from your own side.

SCOREKEEPING

Every beginning bowler seems to think that scoring in bowling is difficult to understand. Many bowlers grow panicky when the job of scorekeeper is suddenly thrust upon them. In many leagues it is customary for the captain to be the scorekeeper, and consequently because it is an honor and a mark of your status to become a captain, it is very important that you learn to score properly. There are some tricks to it, I admit, but once you know the basis for scoring and find that you can do it correctly, there is a great deal of satisfaction in having a well written score sheet, accurately kept. Your teammates, while they may not say it in so many words, will genuinely appreciate your talent.

The secret of scoring in bowling will astound you. You don't add; you subtract. Strange as this statement may seem, it is the trick that makes good scorekeepers.

At least half the time (or more, if you become a really good bowler) you will be "working on the spare". This means that you will be adding a bonus of 10 to the number of pins knocked down on the first ball of the next frame. And here is where the secret comes in: instead of adding 10, add 20 and subtract the number of pins you have left standing.

Example: Working on a spare with 27 in the second frame, you knock down 8 pins. The addition method gives 10 + 8 = 18, to be added to the score of the previous frame; 27 + 18 = 45, and the mathematical steps were difficult, weren't they? Now let's try the trick way: 27 + 20 = 47 (it's easy to add by 10s or 20s), and take away the 2 pins left standing. Answer: 45. Simple, isn't it?

All the traditional talk about how difficult it is to score in bowling, I am convinced, is a result of the natural inability of most people to add their 7's and 8's and 9's, which occur quite often if you add in the old-fashioned way. The other way, the trick method, makes it much simpler, and once you get the hang of it you'll find scorekeeping easy to do. Always remember to ask yourself: "How many pins are left standing?" And you have your answer, whether the bowler has a miss, a spare, or a strike.

Now let me show you that this system works equally well on splits, misses, or strikes.

There are four simple basic situations to understand:

1. If the bowler does not knock down all the pins in two balls, immediately total the number knocked down. By the trick method, in your mind add 10 and take away the number of pins left standing.

2. The spare situation we have just covered.

3. On a strike, you will add to the next two balls the bowler rolls. If the bowler spares in his next frame by knocking down all the pins in two balls, add 10 and 10 for a total of 20. And this immediately suggests that you now learn that spare-strike or strike-spare always means a 20 count added to the first frame, whether spare or strike.

4. The tenth frame is the only unusual frame in scoring. If the bowler scores a strike in his tenth frame he throws two more balls for a total of three. If he makes a spare in the tenth frame, he throws a third ball.

So remember that scoring after a strike is 10 added to the next two balls and scoring after a spare is 10 added to the next one ball. And, if all ten pins are not knocked down in one or two tries, the total number of pins knocked down is entered on the score sheet.

Now, let's score an imaginary bowler for a few frames and see how really simple it is.

Jones bowls his first ball in his first frame and knocks down seven pins. You do not score a total until you see whether he knocks down the three remaining pins on his second ball. Jones misses the three remaining pins. He has scored a miss, or error, and his first frame will show:

Jones	7⊏								

Now let's suppose that he knocked down all three pins on his second ball, which would mean all ten pins down on two balls, or scoring a spare. His score sheet would look like this:

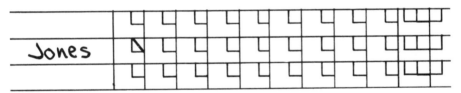

No score is entered because the scorekeeper must wait to see how many pins Jones knocks down on his next ball, which is the first ball of the second frame.

Jones proceeds to throw the first ball of his second frame and knocks down eight pins, leaving two standing. The scorekeeper adds 10 (the scoring bonus for sparing) to 8, the number of pins on the first ball, and then enters 18 in Jones' first frame.

Jones bowls the second ball of his second frame and misses,

leaving the two pins standing. His score is totaled forthwith: 18 on the first frame plus the 8 knocked down in the second frame. His score looks like this:

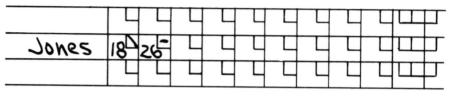

Note that a miss is indicated in the second frame.

Jones proceeds to strike in his third frame, knocks all ten pins down with his first ball. His score sheet now shows:

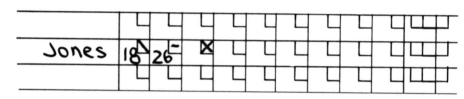

Let's let Jones spare in his fourth frame and strike again in his fifth. Remember: Strike-spare or spare-strike means 20 count, so here's how you score him:

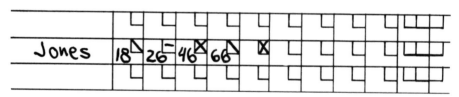

Frame number five remains open until Jones has bowled two more balls. this time he's a hero and strikes each time in frames six and seven. His score now looks like this:

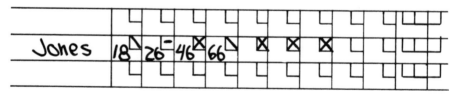

On a string of strikes, bowling superstition says, "Don't mark any score until the string is broken." Actually, when you are ready to score for him in the fifth frame, Jones has earned 30 pins, the 10 bonus plus the total of his next two balls (each 10). So in your mind's eye score him 66 + 30, or 96, in the fifth and wait to see what he does in his eighth frame.

In his eighth frame he draws a wide-open split, the 8-10, and counts one of those pins, the 10 pin. It's an open frame, so you score right through the open frame.

To get Jones' score in the sixth frame you add 10 to his next two balls, which were a strike (10) and 8, the first ball of the eighth frame. Or, by the trick method on a double, add 30 and take away the pins standing after the first ball.

For his seventh frame, you see that he had a "strike up," meaning "wait for two balls before you score." Jones threw two balls in the 8th frame and counted nine. So his score in the 7th frame is now 10 + 9 (or the "trick" way 20 - 1), for 143; and since he did not spare or strike in the eighth, you fill in his score, adding the nine pins he knocked down in the eighth, for 152.

We'll let Jones strike out in the ninth and tenth for a full count; each time he will earn 10 plus the total of his next two balls (10 plus 10), or 30, so his score will look like this:

And you have learned a great deal about scoring. Now for some practical advice, especially useful for team scoring. You will have two bowlers up at a time on right- and left-hand alleys. Get the habit of watching what each bowler has in his previous frame. If one has a spare and the other a strike you know you have to watch the spare bowler's first ball but will wait for two balls from the strike bowler. If one of them is working on a double, be ready to score him through a split or miss with his 30 count, less what pins are left standing—and, above all, be vigilant. Pay attention to your job, for there's nothing more annoying to both bowler and scorekeeper than to hear the question asked, "What did I do in the last frame?"

Your fellow bowlers will love you if you can tell them, "Get a full count for two-oh-four!" and you will if you can learn to score the trick way, shown here.

CHAPTER 13

It is most likely that you will bowl as a regular member of a bowling team and that you will bowl most of your games at one particular bowling establishment.

If you do, you will find that the secretary of your league makes up bowling schedules for all the teams in your league that show on which pair of lanes each team will bowl during the entire season. These schedules are done in a mathematically exact fashion recommended by the American Bowling Congress itself so that each team will face every other team in the league and bowl across all the lanes. Each team is assigned a number. You should obtain one of these schedules before the start of your bowling season and make up your own bowling record sheets for your own personal use.

How to Keep Your Own Bowling Records

I suggest that you use a regular 8½ by 11 inch three-ring binder for this purpose. Your team will be assigned a team number which is then keyed into the schedule of weekly bowling. It will look something like this: (Note: This sample is for an eight team league.)

	Lanes			
	1&2	*3&4*	*5&6*	*7&8*
Sept. 19	1 vs 2	3 vs 4	5 vs 6	7 vs 8
Sept. 26	6 vs 8	5 vs 7	2 vs 4	1 vs 3

Suppose your team has been designated as No. 6. Then you know that you will bowl the first night on lanes 5 and 6, and on lanes 1 and 2 the second night. Break your own lane schedule apart from the general schedule in this manner:

	Lanes	Vs. Team No.
Sept. 19	5 & 6	6
Sept. 26	1 & 2	8

Then add to this the following information which you will keep entering for yourself as your bowling season progresses: your scores, game by game, the number of small and wide-open splits you encounter, how many splits you convert, the number of strikes you get, the number of doubles, and the two totals, the total score for that night and your cumulative score for the season. Finally, you enter your bowling average.

Armed with this information, you accomplish a number of good things from the psychological standpoint. First, you remain constantly aware of what your bowling average is and what scores you need to improve on. You always know your trend toward improvement or not. It will be evident that if you average three misses per bowling session at the start of the season and start missing four or five times later on, you should work harder on making your spares. The same thing holds true about your strike average and your split-conversion average.

I would like to point out to you how important it is that you always know exactly what three-game total will raise your average one pin.

Let's use as an example an imaginary bowler at a point in his mid-season. His record might look something like this:

Lanes	Scores	Strikes	Wide-open Splits	Small Splits	Doubles	Total
Jan. 3 3-4	170/180/160	8	1-0	1-1	2	510
						170-42
						7140

The notation 1-0 under Wide-open Splits indicates that the bowler had one wide-open split and did not convert it. The notation 1-1 under Small Splits indicates that the bowler had one small split and converted it. The notation 170-42 indicates that the bowlers average for 42 games is exactly 170 pins per game. Pins over average or under average are scored as + or -. Under ABC rules the bowler's average is not credited with an extra pin until the total is full, that is, the total pins can be divided by the number of games and give a new higher total.

This bowler looks at his bowling record sheet and knows that he needs a three game total of 510 pins, (3 x 170) to maintain his 170 average. Since he is to bowl his 43rd, 44th, and 45th games, he knows, too, that in order to raise his average to 171 he must bowl not only the three-game total of 170 but also 45 pins over average to give him an average of 171 in 45 games.

His record after the next week would look like this then:

	Lanes	Scores	Strikes	Wide-open Splits	Small Splits	Dbls.	Total
Jan. 3	3-4	170/180/160	8	1-0	1-1	2	510-7140
Jan. 10	7-8	180/190/185	10	0	2-2	4	170-42
							555-7695
							171-45

By the same reasoning, this bowler would also be aware that if he should bowl an extra 45 pins over his average he would raise his average another pin. That would require a pin total of 600 pins to be added to the night of January 3 (510 + 45 + 45) for a total of 7740 (7140 + 600) or 172-45.

My point is this: By keeping your own scoring record and by always being aware of what new pin total you need to raise your average one or two points, you are motivating yourself positively toward your goal of improved bowling.

By examining your scoring record after a number of league nights, you might uncover certain trends in your scores. I know of one bowler to whom I suggested this type of record-keeping, and not long afterward he came to me and said, "Thanks very much for that suggestion. I never knew until I kept those records that I was consistently getting lower scores in my first game than in the other two. Now, I get to the lanes a little early and manage to get a half-game warm-up. Already I've raised my average three pins." If you keep these records for a few years it will give you much satisfaction to look back at your early days of bowling and see your steady improvement in average, in making more strikes per game, fewer misses, and more split conversions.

You should keep your own "book" concerning the lanes your league uses for regular bowling. By this I mean, that you should be constantly aware of the variations that occur in the lanes as you bowl on them. You should not rely upon your memory to register such things as inside or outside angle or a high board; instead you should keep your own personal notebook in which you immediately register your opinion as to the best way for your particular ball to score well on each alley.

I recommend that you get a small three-ring loose-leaf binder about 5 inches by 8, small enough to carry in your bowling bag and yet large enough to use easily. Furthermore, by using the loose-leaf binder, you will find it easier to replace old information with new, up-to-date information as your bowling career proceeds. For example, under ABC rules, bowling lanes must be resurfaced regularly. The result is that information on the way to play certain lanes may be completely outmoded and usually is outmoded by the new lane sanders and resurfacers.

Most of us have a favorite angle on a lane, the one at which the bowling ball "works" the best for us on a lane. So, when you have had a good series on a pair of lanes, write down in your notebook something like this: "Lane 12, used regular line, 10th board, good speed. By third game had to adjust as ball started hitting high. Moved one board left at start, kept same spot. Lane 11, slightly stiffer than 12, had to point ball in first two games, no pointing in last game, just let it go straight away."

Now when you bowl again on Lanes 11 and 12, you have a psychological edge on most of your opponents who will probably not be paying as much attention as you do to the lane conditions. You know that the next time you roll on those same lanes you won't expect to make any unusual changes in your delivery; and knowing that, you are better prepared psychologically to bowl well.

You must not count too heavily on your book, however, as it often happens that a workman who is not paying strict attention to his business of lane preparation can change conditions radically for you. Fortunately, most lane operators insist on uniform preparation of lane surfaces. Besides, modern technology has given us machines now that do the work in a much more uniform manner than an individual could ever do with pushbrooms and Flit-type spray guns, which was the way lanes were conditioned in the old days before modern pin-setting machines were invented.

Another tip I'd like to suggest to you is that you observe other bowlers who roll bowling balls with similar action to that of yours. Without being too obvious about it you can use another bowler's experience on the lanes to help you solve them, too. Let's say that all the outside line bowlers on a pair of teams are scoring well on a particular night while the inside line bowlers are not. That would be a signal to you that you should first try the outside line on those lanes, and it is likely that you would "find the lanes" immediately. Again, this is a psychological benefit for you, one that could add a mark or two to your average a night and thus increase your bowling ability and bowling pleasure.

CHAPTER 14

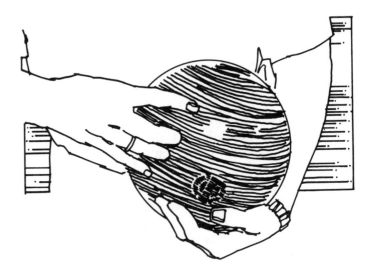

The etiquette of bowling is based upon everyday rules of common politeness. If you are bowling on a team, it is important to arrive at the bowling lane on time. If you know you will be unable to bowl because of sickness or other good reason, by all means call your captain ahead of time so that he can arrange for a substitute to bowl in your place.

If you are bowling on a team and in a match, even an informal one, it is polite to show enthusiasm for your team members' good bowling, their strikes, their difficult spare or split conversions. Pep and chatter in a team win more matches than you may realize. Once the team that halfway through the game is a great number of marks behind begins to chop away at the deficit, the leading team starts to try harder and invariably loses

The Etiquette of Bowling

some of its lead and often is squeezed out in the tenth frame. So be enthusiastic even when the tide rolls against you and your team.

Some of the niceties and fine points in bowling the individual game are based upon sensible rules. The most important main rule is that the bowler, right or left, who has his spare to shoot, has the right of way over the bowler who has a full setup of ten pins to knock down. So defer to your opponent who has his second ball to roll. Should he motion you to go ahead anyway, you are perfectly free to do so. He may want another minute or so to contemplate his spare.

Oddly enough, there is a bit of superstition in bowling which applies when a bowler has a split left standing. There is an unwritten rule that if a bowler on a pair of lanes has a split left, he will immediately clear it away so that the bowler with the full setup does not have to look at it while bowling his first ball.

When both bowlers are rolling first balls, or each one is bowling at a spare, the bowler on the right has the honor to proceed. Sometimes the presence of other bowlers on other nearby alleys will cause a bowler some distraction, so he will motion to his opponent to go ahead. Use good sense and you'll be right most of the time.

Just as in any other sport, a good sport congratulates his opponent on his strikes and good conversions. It is highly improper to needle an opponent or an opposing team with taunts or comments on misses or splits. The best way to upset an opponent or an opposing team is to get a string of strikes for yourself or your team.

It is most important for each bowler to realize that usually he and he alone is interested in how well or how badly he bowls. Consequently, exhibitions of temper or complaints about alley conditions or luck are in extremely bad taste. Remember that good luck usually is counterbalanced by bad luck, and when you have a run of bad luck, be patient. Sooner or later, perhaps even the next time you bowl, you will get that lucky hit in between two strikes so that you can "steal a triple," or three strikes in a row.

For the very same reason—self-interest in bowling—do not offer free advice to any bowler before he asks for it. One of the top bowling teams in the country has a strict rule that no one is allowed to make a suggestion to another team member without permission of the team captain, and he rarely grants permission except in extreme necessity. The reason for this rule, which should be observed by all team bowlers, is that the bowler who is bowling badly becomes more confused than ever when criticism or suggestion for correction is offered. First, he has already probably made several attempts at correcting himself, and on top of his own correction will come perhaps a radically different one. There are many ways to correct a bowler, by slowing him down, by speeding him up, by moving him one way or the other, and possibly the offered correction is entirely wrong. The best advice, if advice must be given, is "Take your time," which really is more of a psychological correction, good advice no matter what he is doing wrong.

CHAPTER 15

Here are some of the most common faults in bowling.

SIDE-WHEELING

Side-wheeling is the name given to a bowler's fault which is caused by the bowler turning his body away from the necessary squareness to the line. By turning clockwise with his body, the bowler causes the ball to come around behind his body. At the delivery point the ball is thrown with the elbow out away from the bowler's body, causing an overturning action with the fingers on top of the ball in no position to impart the necessary lift to the ball. The ball comes off the thumb in this situation and has

Common Faults in Bowling

no action at all. Frequently this type of hand action will cause a sore thumb, for all the weight of the ball is thrown against the bowler's thumb instead of remaining in the fingers where it can be controlled in a proper delivery. The spin of the ball off the thumb may cause severe wear to the thumb. It is a sure sign of an improper delivery.

TAKING THE BALL OUTSIDE

Another major fault the bowler must avoid is the opposite of side-wheeling. Taking the ball outside is caused by taking the ball in its backswing in a definite outside arc. The result is that

Side-wheeling

Taking the
ball outside

128

the elbow strays from its proper position tight alongside the bowler's side. As the downswing progresses, the ball is forced to roll on a line which crosses inwardly and to the left of the headpin. Although some action can be imparted to the ball at the delivery point, usually a bad hit to the left of the headpin results, and sometimes a split will pop up. Quite often, too, this type of fault will result in a "topped" action at the delivery point with the fingers ahead of their proper position and consequently in no position to work properly to impart action to the ball. Most importantly, with this fault the bowler simply cannot roll his ball down his proper line.

SLANTING AND THE WANDERING ELBOW

It is most important that you not let your arm, hand, and bowling ball get out and away from your body at the delivery point. This fault is usually caused by an erratic approach by the bowler called slanting. First, he slants in toward the center of the lane, and then, realizing that he is getting out of position for a suitable delivery, makes either one or the other of two mistakes. If he maintains his approach to the left, he delivers his ball on a line to the left and not on his intended line. Or, if he realizes that he has slanted in and still wants to roll down his intended line, he must let his arm wander out from his body in the illustrated position away from the left foot at the delivery point. From this body position little or no action can be imparted to the ball. The solution is to perfect your footwork so that you are not forced into this situation that leads to bad scores.

RUSHING THE LINE

Charming Mary Last is pictured as she is about to deliver her bowling ball. Note that her sliding foot is turned clockwise to the foul line. This is a certain indication that she has committed a common fault of both male and female bowlers, rushing the line. Mary has bowled in the 145 average class for years but confesses that her trouble has always been caused by this fault. Every bowler should check the position of his sliding foot after he has made his delivery to make certain that he has slid into his intended spot, that he has slid straight toward his target. The turned foot is the telltale sign of a rushed delivery. This fault leads to dropping the ball at the moment of delivery, the body having got out of coordination with the swing and arriving ahead of it. The bowler "dumps" the bowl too short on the lane or even on the foul line.

Slanting and the wandering elbow

Mary Last

CHAPTER 16

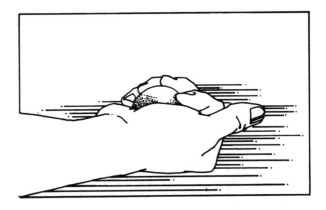

I am firm believer in physical exercise in order to keep my body in as perfect condition as possible. As you know, the Professional Bowling Tour requires that a bowler roll twelve to sixteen games a day for four days with morning and evening sessions. It is not unusual for a professional bowler to bowl 100 games a week in practice when not competing, or in practice and in tournament bowling.

The first requirement for a well conditioned bowler, other than overall physical stamina, is that the bowler's legs be strong. I recommend that every bowler use leg-strengthening exercises. Some bowlers lift weights; others put weighted cuffs on their ankles to strengthen their leg muscles. I recommend walking at a good pace at least two miles a day. Jogging is good, too, but I

Better Bowling and Your Body

feel that you must like jogging a great deal to do it. For me, it is boring and I think that I get as good results from walking as I would from jogging. I ride a bicycle, too, when the weather is good. When it is bad, I use an exercycle at home. On the road I often find an exercise room near the bowling lanes and use it to advantage.

Hand and finger exercises are most important. It will take the average bowler several months or more to bring his hands and fingers to sufficient strength so that he can comfortably handle and control a semi-fingertip bowling ball not to mention a full fingertip ball. It may take a year of such exercises to learn to handle a full fingertip ball. In fact, many bowler's hands are simply not strong enough to handle the full fingertip ball no matter how much exercise is devoted to strengthening them. So I believe that every bowler should be constantly working on strengthening his fingers, hands, and arms.

There are many simple exercises that every bowler can do regularly. If you want to improve your bowling scores, you *must* exercise those muscles which are used in the bowling delivery.

A simple isometric exercise to strengthen the fingers is to press your fingertips together and hold them thus for seven seconds counting "One thousand and one, one thousand and two" and so on. At least once a day you should carry out this exercise. You need great finger strength in order to impart action to the ball and with intelligent exercise you can build your strength up to great capacities.

The use of a simple rubber ball for the palm and fingers is a great way to strengthen your bowling hand. Keep such a ball on the seat of your car, another in your desk drawer, another in the pocket of a coat. Use it faithfully every day. Adopt the isometric theory of full muscle tension for seven consecutive seconds. Clench the ball in your hand and hold it as tightly as possible as you count "One thousand and one, one thousand and two," and so on to one thousand and seven.

Better still get a rubber ball small enough to fit your hand in a simulation of the beginning clenched position of your bowling grip. Practice squeezing it with your thumb relaxed, energizing only the muscles which activate your last three fingers. Feel your lifting motion from the 5 o'clock to 11 o'clock position on the clock dial (see below). Do this exercise from 10 to 20 times a day.

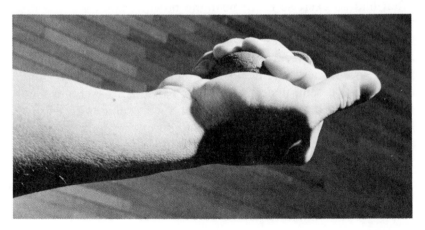

This is a view of the clenched third, fourth and fifth fingers around the rubber ball after you have performed the mock "lift" of your ball. This motion of your fingers should be sudden and the fingers should be held tightly in the clenched position after the action is completed. The muscles on the inside of the arm should be tense, holding the fingers in closed position. The thumb should be relaxed and pointing toward the inside of the imaginary lane.

A wrist-strengthening exercise I have used for years and one that you, too, can easily practice is this: With your third, fourth, and fifth fingers of your bowling hand curved in a mock bowling grip, force them against the resisting left hand as shown in the photograph below. Count seven seconds as "One thousand and one, one thousand and two" and so on. You will find that your wrist and fingers will be remarkably strengthened by this exercise if you will carry it out daily. You can also perform this exercise while sitting at your desk or at the steering wheel of your car. Press straight upward against the desk or steering wheel with the hooked third finger of your right hand. Once more count off those seven seconds as you do this isometric exercise. This exercise will not only strengthen your fingers and wrist, but it will also tighten your abdominal muscles.

You may buy some small barbells with varying weights and use them to add strength to your arms. I recommend ten-pound weights for this purpose, although you should have additional five-pound weights available to allow you to accustom your arm and shoulder muscles to the full weight of the swinging bowling ball.

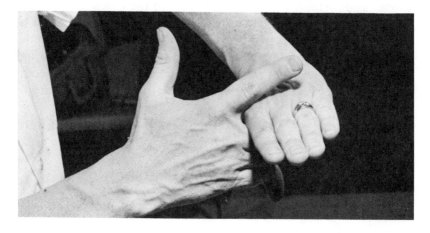

Using the ten-pound weights I suggest that you do "curl" exercises. Taking the bar in your bowling hand, hold it at arm's length straight out in front of you. You may have to start with the five-pound hand weight until your hand and arm becomes strong enough to handle the heavier weight with the weight in front of you. Turn ("curl") your hand and the weight downward and away from you, then return your hand and wrist to the beginning position and do the same exercise again. In time you should build up to about 20 "curls." You will quickly notice a big improvement in your hand and wrist strength. This strength will help you to avoid the bad tendency of breaking your wrist in the backswing of your bowling delivery.

THE PHYSIOLOGY OF BOWLING

I believe that if you understand how your body works in the physical act of delivering the bowling ball you will better understand why I tell you that you must perform certain bodily actions in order to succeed at bowling.

The first demonstration is this: Stand upright before a full-length mirror. Put your right arm down to your side as if it is holding an imaginary bowling ball. Now, while you are still standing and remaining upright, begin to move your arm in an imaginary backswing. Before your arm has gone back 14 to 18 inches, you will begin to feel extreme tension in the muscles of your right shoulder. Furthermore, very quickly as you keep moving your arm backward, you will reach a point at which you cannot comfortably move it any further in the mock backswing.

Now, for the second part of this demonstration, I want you to begin to lean or bend forward at the waist slowly as you do the same backward motion with your bowling arm. You will find that you are able to move the arm backward much more comfortably than you could when you were standing in the upright position.

Conclusion: It is absolutely necessary that you lean forward as you proceed through your bowling delivery. As you practice your bowling you will develop your own "lean forward" style. Most bowlers do it in a gradual fashion, starting from the upright position and ending in a pronounced forward bend as their sliding leg and bent knee takes them closer to the lane at the foul line.

Here is the second physical demonstration I would like you to perform. It will prove to you two things that, in my opinion, are most important for a successful bowling delivery. First, it will show you why you must not let your right elbow wander out from your side; and second, why you must break your arm and wrist directly forward as you deliver the bowling ball.

Here is the demonstration: Take your left hand and grip your right wrist tightly. Try to turn your right wrist counterclockwise by using the wrist hinge alone. You cannot do it! Now let the right wrist turn and see where the turning movement comes from. From the elbow socket and from the shoulder as the elbow and arm leave the side of the body.

These physical demonstrations provide a strong anatomical basis for my claim that in the ideal bowling delivery the elbow, acting as a hinge, is broken directly upward in a plane perpendicular to the floor. Furthermore, you now understand why it is necessary for you to lean forward from the waist as you deliver the ball out over the foul line.

These demonstrations also give you substantiation for my claim that it is necessary for you to remain "square to your bowling line." You will be aided in remaining square when your elbow stays tight to your right side and is not allowed to stray from your body and thus permit undersirable wrist rotation at the moment of delivery.

CHAPTER 17

As you well know, I have bowled hundreds of times in clutch situations, ones where I knew I had to bowl well in order to stay alive in a tournament. Fortunately, I have been able to perform well under these circumstances. Not always, but in a good percentage of them.

Let's talk about pressure in bowling. We all know what it is. We have seen monumental blow-ups in all sports, baseball outfielders who drop simple fly balls, golfers who hook out of bounds on the 18th hole of the last round, big tennis stars who double fault on their serves with television cameras on them—all errrors committed under the pressure of an important World Series game, a U. S. Open golf tournament, a Wimbledon tennis championship.

I would define pressure in sport as that unmistakable tension

How to Make a Strike
When You Need One

that affects the human mind and body under certain circumstances in which there is head-to-head or team-to-team competition for a much desired victory. A money reward is often involved, but on the other hand oftentimes it is merely a sought after honor such as an amateur championship title.

In bowling, as in all sports, the symptoms are subjective, that is, each bowler recognizes the signs in himself. He thinks of how much he wants to win this certain match. His breathing becomes a little different, he takes deep breaths as if he were going to sigh, his hands perspire, he is abnormally thirsty, he finds himself fumbling to tie his shoelaces, he doesn't seem to be able to concentrate. And, there is pressure tension in the muscles of his body.

I believe that all these symptoms are normal, that every good competitor feels them, some more than others. It is my hope that I can explain to you my methods for overcoming pressure in my own bowling game so that you can adapt them to yours and be equally as successful.

THE THREE C's
CONCENTRATION, CONSISTENCY AND CONFIDENCE

If you have ever watched me bowl in one of the televised matches sponsored by the Professional Bowlers Association, you have undoubtedly noticed that I am what you would certainly call a serious bowler. My face is a study in concentration. You might pass your hand before my eyes and not see me blink. Truly, I feel that I have become a master of my own concentration on the task at hand: the solution of the particular pair of lanes on which I must soon begin to bowl and out-score my opponent.

I recommend that you, too, begin to work on your concentration while bowling. Here are some of the things you must have under the control of your mind and your emotions if you are going to bowl successfully. First, you must be thinking of the most important positive side of your game. For me, that is that I maintain my customary speed. I do not want to be forced to change my speed until I have exhausted the other alternatives by changing my ball or angle. So I am concentrating on my "muscle memory" of the timing in my bowling delivery. Just as if I have a television camera filming every move, I can see myself going through all the motions starting with placing my target foot at its proper spot, of sighting over my bowling ball out onto the lane to the arrow I intend to try in my first frame of bowling. By keeping these thoughts in my mind, I am able to block out other distracting thoughts that may try to enter my mind.

Most of all, I try not to think of what I "want" to do and do try to think of what I *am* going to do. This is my way of thinking positively. With a positive thought in my mind, a negative one cannot enter.

How did I develop my power of concentration? In the same way I want you to develop yours. By working at it under every possible circumstance. I found that when I practiced bowling all alone in a bowling lane I could really concentrate on any one phase of my style. Then I found that as other bowlers came in and began to bowl on other lanes, my concentration would slip. I would be distracted by their conversations, by the crash of their strikes. So I made it a game with myself to see whether or not I could bowl and aim for a certain arrow, watch the ball hit that arrow, or not hit it sometimes, and, although being aware of other noises around me, I would not let them intrude into my mind and concentration until I had performed that one bowling delivery. I discovered that I could do it, and I believe that if you will try to do it also, you may be successful.

I have the feeling that my concentration on a certain target, such as one of the lane marker arrows is like having a powerful searchlight aimed at it, a searchlight which I control and with determination can keep in control until I release it once the assigned task, hitting the target, is completed. I believe that it is impossible to concentrate 100 percent of the time, but I also firmly believe that it is possible to concentrate for a good percentage of the time. I have no idea what that percentage is, and it will vary depending upon how powerful the outside distractions are.

I recommend that you work on your concentration the way I have. When you are practicing your bowling you might tell yourself, for example: "From the moment I pick up my bowling ball from the return back, I am going to think of nothing else than the line which goes straight through the 10 board, the second arrow. Then I keep track of what happens mentally as I go to bowl my next frame." Be an outside observer of your own mind. Don't let it wander into other thoughts. If it does, yank it back and "see that line" that you want to burn into your mind.

You will agree, I am sure, that descriptions of mental acts are difficult to accomplish. I hope that I have been able to give you a glimpse inside my mind. You can concentrate, too, on yours with mental practice. Concentration is one of the three big C's as far as I am concerned.

Consistency

The second of the three big C's is consistency. By consistency in bowling I mean a true adherence to the dictionary definition of the word "showing no significant change or unevenness, conforming to the same course of action."

In my opinion, after concentration has been achieved in bowling, it is necessary to obtain consistency in bowling method and in bowling delivery. Let us examine a few of the ways in which the bowler must be consistent in method. The most obvious one is the bowler's grip, for it is the foundation of the entire bowling stroke. The bowler should endeavor to place his fingers into the fingerholes in exactly the same way on every delivery. Most bowlers prefer to insert their action fingers, the third and fourth fingers first and locate them against the sides of the fingerholes with the same degree of inserting and same degree of finger pressure every time.

Then, having inserted the fingers, the bowler places his thumb into the thumb hole, usually with less pressure against the inner sides of the fingerholes. The bowler should try to do this consistently in the same manner every time he grips the ball.

Next, you, the bowler, will assume your stance at the back part of the lane, locating the target spot with your target foot in consistently the same way. That is, you will always place your left toe (or other target foot area such as the inner right-hand sole of the left shoe) at your target dot. From frame to frame you will not move from this dot without having good reason to move, as, for example, to adjust to changing lane conditions. But, once having moved you will consistently return to your new starting spot.

Your grip position, that is, the angle of your fingers in the ball, the straightness of the back of your wrist, your inside-the-bowling-ball finger angle of 5 o'clock to 11 o'clock, or 3 o'clock to 9 o'clock, whatever you have found that gives you the consistent delivery you want—all will also be assembled every time the same way.

Next, your consistency must carry through the mechanics of the delivery. You must push the ball away or drop it away from your body in precisely the same manner every time. Your first true step of the last four must, as we have already pointed out, coincide every time with that pushaway or dropaway, another most important factor in bowling consistency.

Your delivery continues. Your steps are consistently the same length and tempo so that you repeat the same movements of your bowling ball, hand and arm in descending arc, movement of the body forward in its stride, and, at last, the forward arc, the "moment of truth," the precise moment and timing of hand, arm, and bowling ball as you slide toward the foul line perfectly prepared, balanced, and ready to deliver the ball out over the line with a comfortable straight follow-through of the bowling hand and aim.

I am certain that you understand what I mean by the preceding discussion of consistency in bowling. You may say, "I just can't develop that sort of consistency." I say, "Yes, you can. But, you must work hard at developing it."

Confidence

The third of three big C's is confidence. After I have won a particularly hard fought match, I have had many bowling fans come up to me and say, "We knew you were going to win. You had such an air of confidence about you. Your opponent looked very unsure of himself."

It is true that I am a confident bowler in the true meaning of the word according to Webster. I have the feeling that I am "assured of success" when I step out on the approaches against any bowler. I have that feeling most of the time. I hope I will be able to tell you how you can become a confident bowler, too.

We all must face the fact that no athlete can win all the time. There are bound to be moments, even days, when the body simply refuses to perform satisfactorily actions that on other days or stretches of days it performs beautifully and successfully. So, the first thought I want you to consider on confidence is this: "Someone has to be the winner in this match and it might as well be me. I am completely prepared to win and I am *going* to win!" My thought is the positive one rather than the negative one. "I intend to win!" And yours should be the same thought and with the same determination.

You will say, "Will talking about winning help me to win?" I say, "Yes;" provided that you have carried out the many other suggestions I have given you about training yourself to be a better bowler, a winning bowler.

Dr. Robert Nideffer, in his recent book, *The Inner Athlete,* makes the statement that "a relaxed athlete is a confident athlete." I agree with Dr. Nideffer and say that the "relaxed bowler is a confident bowler."

The first foundation stone for that confidence I have, the confidence I want you to build in yourself, lies in your ability to relax, take it easy, move slowly in relaxed fashion, as you deliver your constantly repeating bowling stroke.

I have instructed you on practice techniques and told you how to build that repeating bowling delivery. As you have progressed in making each delivery a carbon copy of the last one and the next one, too, you have come to realize that more and more often you are hitting the pocket and converting more and more spares and splits.

If, at first, your spare and strike average was low, you have seen it go higher and higher as your average kept pace with it. You were "building your odds" as I would say. Understanding that while you might occasionally miss a 10 pin, it was happening so infrequently that you could almost count on making it every time.

At that point in your bowling game there comes the point of relaxation. It came for me and I am confident it will come for you, too. That point is where we understand our percentages of conversion and strike-making and, knowing them, become relaxed because the odds are good to great that we will make certain spares and a certain number of strikes per game.

Through systematic intelligent practice we all develop a natural rhythm in our games. This rhythm helps us to remain relaxed when we are under pressure to win. My own confidence in my ability to bowl well under pressure comes from my conscious attempt not to interrupt my natural rhythm of bowling. I want you to do the same thing with your bowling game. Keep your rhythm! Don't vary it!

Most athletes under pressure tend to move more quickly than they usually do. The golfer jerks his club back quickly in his backswing instead of taking his usual smooth stroke. The basketball free-throw shooter hurries to the line and instead of his usual three or four bounces of the ball before shooting bounces it once and shoots rapidly in an attempt to end his tension as fast as he can.

I consciously attempt to maintain my breathing rhythm as well as the tempo of all my movements from the act of picking up my ball from the ball return rack right on through my bowling delivery itself.

I try to convince myself, and I usually am able to do so, that the strike I need now is no different than the thousands of similar strikes I have knocked down in practice. The pins are the same pins, the lane is the same lane, the bowler is the same bowler. Just because I want the strike does not make any difference.

So, you will be a confident bowler yourself after you have built your bowling style on the sound principles I have suggested, have built your own unhurried, unvaried rhythmic delivery, the foundation of confidence in bowling because it will make you a relaxed bowler who "knows his odds" and cashes them in for strikes!

CHAPTER 18

Obviously, the purpose of bowling is to attain as high a total score as you possibly can. So, let's consider a number of bowling situations that will affect your total score so that you may understand the strategy that applies to them when you encounter them.

The most important rule to remember when bowling against splits is "always count the greatest number of pins you can." Each extra pin knocked down in a split that has three or more pins left standing will count as two in your final score. Here's an example: You have left two pins on the right-hand side and one on the left in the 6-7-10 split. You have a strike up in the preceding frame. If you knock down the 6-pin and 10-pin with your second ball your count will be 19 + 9 = 28; whereas if you

The Strategy of Bowling

knock down only one pin out of the 6-10 leave or choose to shoot for the 7-pin and make it, your score will be 18 + 8 = 26, or two less pins than you would have scored by taking down two pins.

This scoring problem, whether to try to convert the wide-open splits and by missing the conversion lose count is an important one. In general, you should go for the count rather than the conversion because in the long run your average can be affected by as much as a whole pin over the entire season. When a team game is so close that the conversion of a wide-open split may make the difference between winning or losing by one mark (ten pins), the bowler should certainly make his best effort to make the split and win the game. There is no greater thrill for a bowler than to receive the applause of his teammates when he has bravely attacked a wide-open split and, whether by skill or luck, converted it to help win the game. The anticipation of such a thrill is another reason why the bowler should constantly work in practice on making his spares, particularly the 10 pin, because very often the ability to convert the 10 pin carries over to an ability to convert the 6-7-10 wide-open split.

Remember that there is a mathematical chance for you to convert any split which has one or more pins on a line in front of the other or others, offering the opportunity for the ball to clip the front pin on one side and slide it across the lane to take down the other pin or pins. Study the photographs and my analyses of the best methods of converting typical splits and spares, and you will better understand the technique and strategy involved in converting them.

Now let's talk about the strategy of bowling the ninth and tenth frames. You must make every effort to bowl a strike in your ninth frame. Of course, if you can get a strike in your eighth frame as well it is even better. But with a strike in the ninth you are in a desirable scoring position. You may capitalize on it be rolling another strike in the tenth frame. Making your ninth frame strike is called "laying a foundation."

It is said that "You have a strike to work on." You have a chance to "go all the way in the 10th," that is, to get all three strikes in the 10th frame and thus "get a full count." So, often a game that has started with a miss or split can be picked up dramatically with strikes upon strikes in the last frames of the game.

Always remember that it takes one double, that is, two strikes clustered together, to erase the loss of pins from a miss or an unconverted split. So, go after those late frame strikes and cash them in for higher scores.

You may think that I am insisting that you strike in every frame. We both know that this is impossible, but the ball that "almost" gets a strike is usually the ball that is "working" and will leave a simple spare. If you do not strike on your first ball,

148

your goal is to leave no more than one pin in your spare. So, my advice to you is "Never let up." Don't ever loaf or be careless about a delivery. If you do you will find yourself facing difficult spares and leaving splits you can't make.

Let's consider the scores of two bowlers, Jones and Smith, who have the same score, 165, in their eighth frames and we'll let Jones have a ninth frame spare and Smith a strike.

Now, we'll let each bowler strike out in the tenth frame, that is, roll all three strikes.

Here's how the score sheet looks:

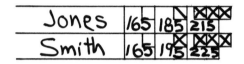

Let's suppose that neither bowler strikes out in his tenth frame. We'll let each one spare in the tenth and then get 10 pins apiece on their final balls.

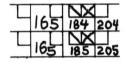

Here is the result: Jones wins again by one pin. Again, a vivid demonstration of the need for that "foundation" strike in the ninth frame for Jones and for you.

Just as the ninth frame is an important one, so too are your first frame and second frames. There is nothing more discouraging to an opponent than to watch you start right off with a strike or even a spare made in authoritative fashion.

You must try never to give any "consolation to your enemy." There is nothing more discouraging in team bowling than to watch your opponents rack up strike after strike, mark after mark in the early part of the game. You know that you are going to have to fight for the victory and you shouldn't even let the thought cross your mind, "Maybe we can't win it!"

CHAPTER 19

I have used personally and continue to use several unusual ideas in practicing my bowling technique. You will recall that I told you earlier about how I would shadow bowl on the lanes and how it helped me improve my game. I believe that you should try shadow bowling, too. Go to your nearby lane manager and find out whether or not he will allow you to shadow bowl instead of bowl at the pins. I believe that he will be happy to accommodate you. With a little persuasion he should cut your cost per bowling line substantially.

I recommend that you develop a definite bowling routine. By this I mean that you should see yourself as an actor-participant in the bowling scene from the moment the bowler who proceeds you has finished his delivery until you have bowled and returned

How to Practice Bowling
at the Lane and at Home

to your seat. See yourself waiting at the scoring table, for instance. Now it is your turn to bowl. See yourself looking to the right and left lanes to make sure that the way is clear for you to proceed. You are unhurried, acting in a leisurely way as you step to the back of the ball rack and pick up your bowling ball.

Now, you start a mental count of seconds as you assemble yourself in your delivery. One thousand-one, one thousand-two, and so on, second by second. You proceed with your mental countdown by placing your left shoe at about the one thousand-four count. You are placing your fingers into the finger holes precisely as you want them to be. Your thumb is inserted last. You are sighting your arrow marker out on the lanes, the line you want to the pins.

You take a deep breath at about the one thousand and ten count, exhale slowly, and, now relaxed, are ready to bowl the frame.

I firmly believe that every bowler will benefit by establishing such a routine and sticking to it. Each bowler must determine for himself the count and timing. I have used the sweep second hand of my watch to note and regularize the timing of my bowling routine.

I suggest that you try it bowling by yourself or else trust a friend of yours to time you as you go through the entire routine of bowling. What you are trying to achieve is this: absolute standardization of every delivery in time and in style, a delivery that will stand up under pressure, one that will be so much second nature to you that you will carry it out automatically.

The result will be a great feeling of control, not only of your bowling delivery but also of your emotions. Let's say that just as you are about to start your pushaway a tremendous shout disturbs your concentration. You stop cold. You will find that having developed your routine you will have such control of your emotions that you will be able to stop your delivery and resume your routine, say, at the point where you place your left foot properly. Then you will proceed with your delivery as if nothing had happened to disturb you.

I recommend that you always bowl in an unhurried fashion. Don't allow anyone to rush you into your delivery. Early in my bowling life I decided that I was missing a lot of spares needlessly by hurrying them. So, I began the habit of making myself wait until my ball had completed its return to the ball rack before I made any effort toward rolling my second ball. It slowed me down and forced me to take more time on my spares. The result was that I made more of them.

You will have to work out your own timing. Some people naturally move faster than others. A rapid bowler cannot slow down his routine too much, and a slower bowler cannot speed up his.

When you eventually work out your routine, I promise you

better scores, more peace of mind, and control of your nerves in your bowling.

When you practice your bowling, I advise you to practice one particular phase of your game during each practice session. For example, let us say that you know you have been troubled with the problem of staying down at the line as you deliver your ball, not following through.

As you mark your score sheet, you should make a particular mark to indicate "I did stay down." No mark would indicate you are continuing your error. At the end of a session you can see what progress you are making in overcoming your fault. You should keep week-to-week records of such practice until you have overcome the fault and are able to stay down every time you roll the ball.

Another excellent practice idea is to note how many times you hit the pocket contrasted with how many times you cross over to the 1-2 pocket. Establish a system of checks to give yourself credit for every pocket hit and none for missed pockets. You might even try head-to-head bowling with another bowler who has the same problem you do, paying each other a nickel or a quarter each time either one of you crosses the headpin. You will soon find that when your fault costs you money, you will pay a great deal more attention to the 1-3 pocket than you ever did before in your bowling.

Here is a method to check whether or not you are releasing your ball at the same spot each time. First, place a piece of carbon paper between two sheets of white paper. Second, with permission from the bowling center owner or manager, place this on the alley in the area where you release the ball and fasten it with scotch tape. Third, make your delivery several times. As the ball hits the paper target, it will leave impressions on the sheet under the carbon, and you can determine whether or not you are dropping the ball at the same spot each time.

Another practice tip I believe you will find useful is this. Try to practice under conditions that are as quiet as possible so that you can concentrate on getting rid of your faults. Most bowling lanes have what are called "dark times," hours of the day between leagues or when no bowlers customarily bowl. I recommend that you check with the bowling proprietors in your neighborhood and ask them for their advice on when you can bowl with them with the least distraction. You can often find that there is a quiet hour at noon or in the late afternoon when there is no league bowling. And, if you make the lane manager your friend you can often persuade him to fill up all the other lanes besides the ones adjacent to you before he finally assigns those lanes which will be most distracting to your practice.

If you are unable to arrange for a regular practice session, I suggest that you attempt to reach your regular bowling league lanes well in advance of the starting time so that you can at least roll a practice game or two ahead of time. The bowling ball is heavy and your arm and body definitely need a physical warm-up before you begin the effort of bowling.

When you practice, I recommend that you keep yourself constantly under pressure. Put up a dollar or so that you will promise to give to charity if you do not spare ten frames in a row. Or, bowling head-to-head with your bowling friends (or enemies), always have a little money on the game, even if it is a quarter a line so as to put yourself under pressure all the time not to miss spares and to get as many strikes and doubles as possible for the highest game score. Only by putting yourself under pressure will you learn to bowl under pressure, and later on, after you have improved your bowling style and mental attitude as a result of some of the tips I have given you, you will bowl *well* under pressure.

You may practice bowling away from the lanes also. Most people these days have a recreation room with a vinyl flooring. If you have one, it is ideal to use for practicing your footwork and bowling approach.

In your recreation room, or for that matter in any room that has a suitable vinyl flooring, you can and should build your own mock bowling practice approach. Get some wax such as is used on dance floors and spread it where you will be making your mock slide. I recommend that you put down a one-inch wide white adhesive tape 12 feet long with a second piece of tape to form cross-bars at each end of the first tape to represent your starting position and an imaginary foul line.

Let this first tape be the center line of your approach. Merely walk it at first and then begin to work on the timing of your steps to the line. Put on your bowling shoes. Pretend you are actually bowling. Hold your imaginary bowling ball and keep your eye on a definite spot beyond the foul line, one that would represent your target arrow on a real bowling lane: then work on timing your pushaway or dropaway to your first step.

Try this experiment. I have found it very useful myself. With your eyes on your target and thus not watching where your first step is taking you, make that first move and then stop and look down to see where in relation to the white line that step has taken you. It should be to the right side of the tape and directly on its straight path toward the imaginary foul line. Mark also how far that step has taken you. Put a mark on the tape so that on your next mock delivery you can tell whether you are taking a step of the same distance or not. With the mark on the tape you have a beginning guide to building yourself a constantly repeating bowling stride, one that is exactly the same, delivery after delivery. You will be laying the foundation for those most important bowling fundamentals, consistency and timing.

An experienced bowler who has practiced intelligently and studiously for a number of years automatically assumes the proper stance, takes the proper grip on his ball, positions his body so that it is square to his intended line, and so forth. He doesn't have to check many of these things because he has built his bowling experience into a total overall feeling of body and mental attitude. Once he has been able to develop this feeling his mind is able to focus on additional matters that might require his attention. It stands to reason that if a bowler is worrying about where he should place his starting target foot to make a particular spare, he cannot at the same time be working on what may be, for him, the most important problem of all, an apparent difference in lane conditions with one lane running more than the other and requiring intense concentration on his part to solve satisfactorily.

My point is that you, too, must practice and practice until you can reduce the simple problems, and even the difficult problems, to as much of an automatic and correct solution as you can. That is why I advise you to learn the pins by "name," really their numbers. Make each one your friend so that you can say, "There you are again, old 10-pin. I don't miss you anymore. Just watch me knock you down!" And then do it!

CHAPTER 20

All bowlers get into trouble. Here are some tips for you when you get into trouble.

Sometimes it seems that no matter how perfectly your strike ball hits the pocket that stubborn 10-pin will remain standing. It happens to all bowlers. It happens to me. The most important advice I can give you is "Don't get upset"! Don't let your blood pressure rise to the point that your physiology changes and you roll your next ball in fury, or roll it so carelessly that you loaf on the shot and miss it. You must learn to accept the breaks of the game whether they come in the form of maddening 10-pins, or 4-pins, or even splits. You must remain calm enough to be able to analyze what happened and to be able to make a sensible, successful adjustment in your bowling method so as to lessen the chances of the same problem recurring.

What to Do When
You Are in Trouble

When you are bowling that first strike ball, remember that if the 3-pin hits the 6-pin too far on the right side of the 6-pin, the 6-pin will go to the left of the 10-pin and miss it. If the 3-pin is moved into the 6-pin too far on the left side of the 6-pin, the 6-pin will go to the right and "wrap around" the 10-pin, leaving the 10-pin again.

So it is most important that your angle of entry into the 1-3 pocket be just right, not too high on the headpin, not too light to its left in order to carry out the proper chain reaction of 3-pin into 6-pin, which then takes out the 10-pin. While you may be lucky enough to get the 10-pin sometimes as a result of other pin action, you must not count on it.

I firmly believe that the major problem that causes 10-pin taps (hits that seem perfect but leave one pin standing) is too much speed on the ball. So my recommendation to you for avoiding 10-pin taps is to slow down your ball somewhat. This solution may be the one that enables you to get the 10-pin instead of leaving it.

If change of speed doesn't work for you, or if the results are not satisfactory, for example, if you start hitting the pins "on the nose" and leaving splits, then I recommend that you change your bowling angle. Try moving a board or so to your left, keeping your customary spot at the arrows. That will bring your ball into the pocket a little "lighter," and it may be the answer. I hope it is for you, it usually is for me.

If you are leaving the 4-pin consistently, my first comment is "congratulations!" for you are hitting the pocket solidly and you are only a fraction of an inch away from a strike. I suggest that you change your speed a little bit. You need to have the ball get to the pocket a little bit later. By speeding it up you will delay its final roll in the hook that tiny amount which should bring it into the pocket enough later to hit the headpin at the proper angle to cause it to take out the 4-pin.

Sometimes the 4-pin is left when the strike ball "dives," or jumps into the headpin too quickly. When this happens you should try to adjust your bowling line so that your ball will "catch the track" a little later. That means one of these two moves for you. Move to your left, or inside your former line, and roll the ball over the same spot you have been using. In this way, your ball will "catch the track" a little later and also act on the 1-3 pocket a little later. The other move is to the extreme right with a delivery which takes the ball outside the track for a certain distance (you must determine that distance by your angle toward the 1-3 pocket) and then allows the ball to "catch the track" short of the pocket.

Keep your eyes on your ball as it nears the pocket. If you watch carefully you can observe the "diving" action, or on the other hand, the failure of your ball to make its proper move into the pocket. I know that these instructions are tricky and intricate. But, the game of ten-pin bowling is not a simple one. If

160

you want to succeed in knocking down ten pins with a consistently working strike ball it is necessary that you experiment with your bowling delivery, your timing, your speed of approach, and speed of the ball itself and that you understand the effect of angling your bowling ball toward the 1-3 pocket. The effort of learning these things pays off in higher bowling scores and a great deal of personal satisfaction at conquering, or almost conquering a very difficult sport.

SPECIAL ADVICE FOR THE ADVANCED BOWLER

Let's assume that you have mastered the fundamentals of bowling. Even so, you will find that there are many subtleties of the bowling approach and delivery that may continue to be a mystery to you. Don't feel that you are alone in this situation. Even the best bowlers have scoring problems at times and have difficulty in solving them.

My best advice to you when you find yourself in trouble is, "Don't fight the lane!" By that I mean that if the lane is running, that is, the ball hooks easily, adjust to that condition rather than fight it. Try one of these solutions as your cure: first, move your starting spot slightly left but continue to use the same target at the arrows; second, try picking a spot farther out on the lane as your target and be sure your follow-through reaches for that spot. By reaching for a more distant target you will be able to get the ball out farther over the foul line and delay its hook at the end of its track. Finally, and only as a last resort, increase the speed of your ball. This is dangerous to do because it may throw your timing off completely. In changing your speed try to accomplish it first by faster hand action and full follow-through at the line. Bring your hand and arm up sharply, keeping your normal tempo of footwork to the line. That may work, but then if it does not you will have to speed your footwork as well as your hand action. If you do change your footwork, try to keep it rhythmic even though a little faster. Don't attempt to take a longer, quicker first step for that may destroy your rhythm. Think "smoothness and rhythm" but visualize yourself in a slightly faster tempo to the line. This is the most difficult adjustment for any bowler to make. It should be done only when all the other corrections in angle and line have been exhausted.

If you feel that you are releasing your ball properly and that under usual conditions it would be hooking and you still can't make your ball "move," then I suggest these adjustments. First, move slightly to the right of your normal starting position. Second, try to slow up your ball slightly so that it will accept more of the traction on the lane. Finally, move your target at the arrow range finders slightly to the left. Sometimes on a particularly stiff lane, you may go in as far as the third range finder.

Sometimes it seems that nothing works for you. When this happens, forget about trying to get strikes. Bowl defensively by trying not to come in on the nose on a running lane, by not missing the headpin on one that is stiff. Sometimes this bowling defensively works miracles. You may lose some tension by not trying for strikes, "accepting your fate," and your ball may start coming to life again and getting the strikes.

Be assured that bad nights of bowling happen to all bowlers. I have had them. You will have them. They are all part of the game. Accept them and be patient until the next good night when all the bad breaks will be balanced with good breaks.

SPEED CONTROL

If you are rolling your ball too fast most of the time, you should shorten your approach by a foot or two in order to reduce your backswing. Many great bowlers, Buzz Fazio, for example, consistently roll from a normal three-step starting spot. Junie McMahon, another great bowler, had almost no backswing and yet scored sensationally.

If your ball is too slow most of the time, you should increase the height of your backswing. You can do this by a slightly higher pushaway or dropaway. Sometimes, too, a ball only a pound lighter than the one you are accustomed to will prove to be the answer to your getting more speed.

If you are bothered with drifting to the right or left in your approach and cannot correct it by the method I have suggested for building a straight approach, then you should build in the necessary corrections to compensate for it. If you drift right, keep your first step more to the left than would be normal for your approach. If you drift left, try the reverse strategy, by stepping off to the right on your first step. Of the two faults, drifting left is the more serious because it is inclined to give you less leverage at the line; and in an effort to correct the fault at the last second, it may cause faulty hand action at the line as you attempt to go straight down a bowling line you are really crossing as you come in from the right side.

A right drift is less serious and can actually result in more leverage at the line because the hand and arm are brought close to the sliding foot.

To get added speed on the ball and as result, less hooking action, just bring your hand up a bit faster at the release than you normally do. You should also add a little extra effort to your follow-through.

To slow your ball just a trifle, you should do the reverse: just don't bring your hand up at the release very hard at all and leave almost all of the snap out of your hand as it lets the ball go.

CHAPTER 21

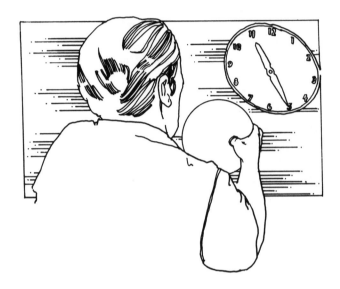

I perform several physical actions when I bowl that other good bowlers do not do. In my opinion, some of these actions, perhaps all of them, contribute to my bowling success. Possibly I would have succeeded as a professional bowler without these changes in my basic delivery. What I do know is that with these individual "Anthony variations," I have been able to win under almost any and all lane conditions.

I do not know whether you will be able to adopt any of these modifications into your bowling style. I assure you that it took me, personally, hundreds upon hundreds of hours of practice to perfect them for myself. I am certain that if you wish to perform any of them yourself it will take you, too, many hours of intelligent practice and experimentation. But if you do achieve the ability to do some of these things that I will now discuss, I as-

My Super-Secrets for
Better Bowlers

sure you that your bowling will improve. It might even improve sensationally.

The instructions that I now propose to give should be of interest to the male bowler who is presently averaging, I would say, in the neighborhood of 165 or a comparable average 150 for a woman. For I feel that the bowlers of either sex who are scoring that well at this time have already learned the basics of bowling and have developed an individual style that is repeating frame by frame. It is also true, I feel, that if the bowler should happen to be scoring in the higher ranges now than the 165-150 man-woman range, his chances for success are even greater. I do make this strong statement now: you *will* improve your bowling average if you are able to adopt even one of the special Anthony super-secrets.

THE TURNED-OUT SLIDING FOOT

Your sliding foot does not necessarily slide straight forward with your line of delivery!

I do not remember what it was that caused me to experiment with the direction of my sliding foot. When I was a beginning bowler I often found that I rushed the line and my sliding foot ended up turned away from the pins in what might be said to be an 11 o'clock position. I began to concentrate on watching my sliding foot, forcing it to slide straight along the line toward the pins I wanted. Remember that I was shadow-bowling those hundreds of games per week when I was trying to get myself up into the 200 average class of bowlers. Somehow it happened that in practice I rolled a particularly powerful ball at one time and looked down to see where my sliding foot had ended near the foul line. I was surprised to see that instead of being straight it had ended at an angle away from the pins, in what would be about 11 o'clock position.

I tried the delivery again, this time consciously thinking about my slide and trying to sense where in the final part of the slide I was getting my sliding foot into the 11 o'clock position. I had many failures, but the fact remained that when I was able to turn my heel inward and, of course, my toe outward at that last second of my slide, I was getting a great deal more lift on my ball. I was quite excited about this discovery and kept it to myself. As I continued to practice the trick and use it when I wanted a particularly strong ball, the technique worked. I will be telling you later on when and how you can use this Anthony "trick." For now bear with me as I explain what I call my other super-secrets. The turned-out sliding foot is the first one.

The First Super-Secret, the Turned-Out Sliding Foot

Approximately one second before you reach the end of your slide, gradually start to turn your sliding foot counterclockwise,

The turned-out sliding foot

that is, to the left of the headpin. When you finish your slide, your sliding foot should be aiming at about 11 o'clock on a clock dial. The result is that your body weight is thrown even more to the left than usual, and as your hand comes up from behind you will find that you are able to put more leverage into the shot and get more action on the ball.

THE SECOND SUPER-SECRET: THE 11 O'CLOCK SHOT

Here is the second super-secret of my bowling. When you want less action on your bowling ball, your armswing should be on an 11 o'clock to 5 o'clock axis on the backswing.

As it often happens with beginning bowlers, especially natural left-handers such as I was and am, my natural ball broke sharply at the pins most of the time. While a good strong, sharp break at the pocket is most desirable, of course, on some occasions it can get you into serious trouble. That happens when the lanes are running and helping your ball to break at the last moment. Lane conditioning or increasing dust on the lane surface oftentimes will cause a slower track and make the ball react more quickly as it comes into the strike area. The result is a ball that breaks too quickly, hits the nose of the pin setup, or even crosses over the headpin and may or may not hit the left hand, or Brooklyn, side of the pins. The final result may be a lucky strike on some occasions, but more often there is a bad leave or even a split.

So, with my strong ball I found that I was fighting to stay in the pocket in the latter stages of good games. I was looking for a solution for myself, something that would delay my hit a fraction of a second longer. It happened that I was bowling along with a poor bowler whose ball was carrying the kind of strikes I wanted. I watched him in amazement. He had what bowlers call a "nothing ball." And yet, he was knocking down the pins. I studied his delivery and realized that he had what, at that time, I believed was a basic flaw. His arm swing was not at a true right angle to his body and line to the pins. He was pushing his ball in toward the center of the lane and then bringing his arm on the outside of his body on his backswing. I had to give him some credit, though. He was returning the ball on the same plane or line of delivery on which he started his backswing.

I resolved to try his method myself in practice to see whether I could "kill" my ball the same way. So the next practice session I had, I began to experiment with my pushaway, putting the ball one time three or four degrees toward the headpin and then on another occasion, even more angled in toward the headpin. At last, I found what was for me a marvelous solution. I could put the ball in about on an 11 o'clock - 5 o'clock axis and roll an almost perfectly straight ball. It had just a little final snap at the pins. Furthermore, I discovered that by not aiming that axis quite so far left of the headpin, I could partially "kill" my ball. Good bowlers will recognize that I also had to refrain from putting as much lift on my ball as usual. But, I found that easy to do. My hand was in a less favorable position to put on lift when it was on the side of the ball in a slightly broken wrist position. This is a very delicate shot because the fingers dare not pass the

168

thumb at the moment of delivery or I would have an over-turned ball with either no action at all or even a back-up, left-to-right action, which is definitely undesirable. All I can say is that by assiduous practice I have been able to master this shot. I think that the good bowler can do so as well if he will really work at it and understand what he is trying to do. It is invaluable on extremely running lanes. I call it my second super-secret.

The 11 o'clock shot

The Second Super-Secret: The 11 O'clock Shot

In this shot I keep my body square to my intended line, but I visualize a clock dial with the hands at 11 o'clock and 5 o'clock. Then I put the ball on that eleven o'clock axis and back toward 5 o'clock. The result is that my ball is farther away from my body than usual, and I get less action on the ball at the delivery point. This is coupled with a breaking of my wrist downwardly, flattening it, it is called; and the result is a ball with very little action until the very end of the shot. It is invaluable to me on extremely running lanes where I want to delay my hit.

169

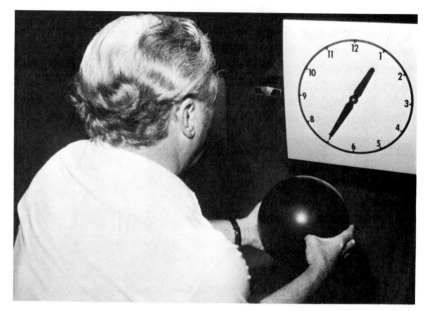

The one o'clock shot

THE ONE O'CLOCK SHOT

This is another one of my secrets for putting more power into a shot. I keep my body square to my intended line but I visualize a clock dial set at 1 o'clock and 7 o'clock. Then I put my ball on that axis. The result is that my arm remains even closer than usual to my body, and the ball at delivery point is close to my sliding foot. I find that I have more leverage on the ball when it comes from that position. This trick combined with my turned-in sliding foot really gives me considerably more power than usual.

THE CERTIFIED BOWLING COACH

Here is one more super-secret to improve your bowling. It is very likely that there is a certified bowling coach in your area. I recommend strongly that you consult him or her about your bowling problems and bowling style. If you do you will be a more satisfied bowler as he or she can put you on the road to improvement and higher scores.

Just as the Professional Golfers Association conducts a school for its players to qualify for competition so, too, does the United States Bowling Association carry out a certification program for approved bowling coaches.

The program began in 1992 in anticipation of the declaration by the Olympic Committee that the sport of bowling would be included among those in the next Olympics. Under Olympic rules each sport is required to have certified coaches.

The bowling qualifying school was held for the first time in Tampa, Florida. Twenty-five bowlers paid entry fees of $400 each. At the end of the course three types of certifications were issued to the successful candidates. A coach with "Bronze" certification is one authorized to teach bowlers with an average of 165 or less. A "Silver" coach is one qualified to teach bowlers averaging 210 or more, and he or she must be proficient in drilling and laying out a bowling ball. A "Gold" coach must have all the foregoing abilities and also be knowledgeable in sports psychology and the advanced mathematics of bowling.

Call your local Bowling Association for more information on finding a certified bowling coach near you.

CHAPTER 22

Aside from the ball, shoes, and standard bag (all covered earlier in the book), there are some new pieces of equipment to help the bowler improve his game. They can add convenience to the bowler's life, too.

WRIST PROTECTORS

There are many different kinds of gloves and appliances meant to be worn to keep the bowler's wrist from breaking down at the delivery point and to allow a consistent, repeating bowling delivery.

I recommend the Pro Release over all others. This wrist protec-

New Bowling Equipment

tor is engineered in such a way that the bowler can actually adjust it to give him the breaking ball he desires, from straight to a strong hook. That is, if he wants a strong hook at the end of his roll, he clicks a lever a couple of notches to the left and, lo and behold, he has the result he wants.

The Pro Release wrist protector is good for all bowlers, especially the beginning bowler who usually needs help to keep his wrist from breaking down in the backswing or at the delivery point. The Pro Release is relatively expensive, about $50, but well worth the expense. It will definitely help you to raise your scores.

On the following page are two views of the Pro Release wrist protector.

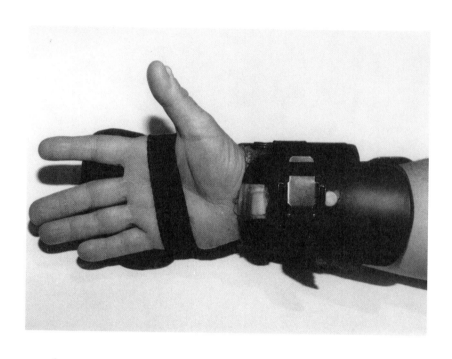

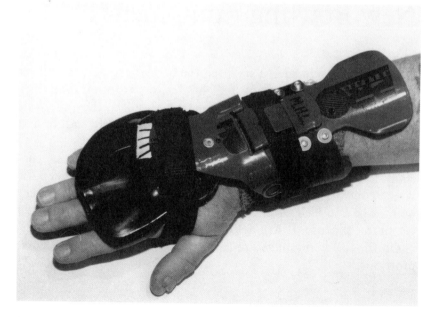

BALL CARRIERS

Bowlers now carry more than one bowling ball to the lanes in anticipation of various lane conditions. The top photo shows some of the new ball-carrying bags and devices. The bags on the left handle two balls each. Note the kit with space for six different balls. The bowler needs a great deal of strength for this "six-pack," but it does come with its own set of wheels like a piece of luggage.

FINGER-HOLE INSERTS

Here Dawson Taylor demonstrates the finger-hole inserts that cushion the bowler's fingers and give a firmer, non-slip grip on the ball for a consistent delivery. These inserts, made of plastic, are an excellent way to prevent the formation of blisters on the thumb or fingers.

175

CHAPTER 23

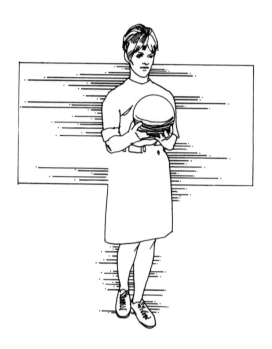

The women of America have taken up bowling enthusiastically during the last three decades. At one time a bowling alley was considered a dirty smoky place where mostly men got their recreation and their night out away from their wives. Now, the alley is a lane, and it is clean with the air constantly refreshed by modern air conditioning. More than 3,500,000 American women bowl in regularly scheduled leagues, and undoubtedly another 1,000,000 bowl with their husbands, families, and friends for recreation.

No matter what the Womens' Liberation movement of today may claim, we must face the fact that women are simply not the physical counterparts of men when it comes to lifting, handling, and rolling with authority the heaviest allowable bowling ball,

Bowling for Women

the 16-pounder. Therefore, I recommend that women bowlers in choosing the weight of a bowling ball first consider the question of control. If you are unable to lift comfortably a ball weighing more than, say, 10 or 11 pounds, then you have your answer: use a ball that weighs no more than that.

If, on the other hand, you find that such a ball feels light (it may, of course), then I suggest that you start to experiment with slightly heavier balls to see whether or not you can handle them with ease and, most importantly, with control.

The manager of the bowling lane can explain to you the code imprinted on the house bowling balls so that you will know how heavy a particular ball is. If you start with a 10-pound ball, move up one pound to an 11-pound ball. Stay with it for a while and then try a ball that is another pound heavier. You will have to decide yourself when you start to have difficulty controlling the ball.

I do not want you to have the feeling that the ball is controlling you; that will sometimes happen when a bowler tries to use a ball that has more weight than the bowler can control. Incidentally, it is not unusual to see this same lack of control in men bowlers also as a result of using too heavy a bowling ball. Such men are foolishly proud in being unwilling to face the fact that they may not be physically strong enough to use the 16-pound ball either.

So, determine the ball weight that suits you and use it. Of course, you and I both understand that the heavier ball obeys the laws of physics and exerts more force on the bowling pins and will carry more hits than a light ball will. But there is that certain point which you must find for yourself at which added weight no longer means added explosive power at the pins but rather a lowering of the score as a result of lack of control.

I will make an educated guess and state that most women bowlers do not use 16-pound bowling balls but use bowling balls in the 12- to 14-pound range instead.

One result of bowling with the lighter ball is that the woman bowler must use more angle, that is, her ball must come in more from the right-hand corner than from the right center of the lane. By using this angle the woman bowler is enabled to attack the 5-pin more directly. While her ball because of its lighter weight will be subject to more deflections to the right as the ball enters the 1-3 pocket, still the increased angle will help her to counteract the deflection, spill all the pins, and rescue her from the nasty 5-7 split so indicative of the weak strike ball.

The same advice I have given to the men bowlers about grip and ball balance applies to women bowlers. A woman's skin may be, and probably is as a general rule, softer and more easily rubbed or blistered than a man's. Therefore, I recommend that all women bowlers use a wrist support for better scoring success.

Besides, women's wrists are not as strong as men's and the

weight of the bowling ball is inclined to cause the wrist to break either downward or into a flat position. Usually when the wrist breaks in the backswing, it is almost impossible for a bowler, even a good one, to regain the proper hand position, an unbroken wrist at the delivery point. The bowling glove with its wrist supports will help you to avoid the fault of the wrist-break. You will bowl a more consistent ball and will score better.

If you have a bowling ball that properly fits your hand, one that has individual finger spans that allow your thumb to release easily at the proper moment and your fingers to stay in the ball that fraction of a second longer so as to impart the proper lift as you deliver the ball out over the foul line, you are on your way to bowling success.

In my opinion, too many women bowlers attempt to bowl "beautifully," that is, put on a dignified show of athletic ability. I do not believe that bowling is a suitable game for especially dignified conduct. It is a game that does require considerable physical effort, and if more attention is given to how the bowler looks in her delivery rather than the question of "how I am going to bowl this bowling ball so as to knock down ten pins in one strike," then the bowling score will suffer. So I advise you to get rid of your inhibitions and let the ball fly down the lane with authority. Don't be ashamed to exhibit some "body English," or gyrations, after the ball is on its way. But make sure that you have completed your full follow-through before you consider any "help" for the ball on its way to the pins. And keep your body actions confined to your own lane so that you won't distract or upset nearby bowlers, won't you?

There is no doubt, either, but that some women are physically able to handle and control well the maximum weight of a 16-pound ball. If you are blessed with good height and a strong physique, then I recommend that you try to use the 16-pound ball. You may like it and find that it does not tire your hand and arm too much for you to bowl with it. You will be one of the lucky women bowlers, able to meet the men and possibly beat them on their own terms.

Cherile Graham

Here I am instructing Cherile Graham, a fine bowler in the Tacoma area. Cherile is a good-sized girl and rolls a 16-pound ball with ease. She has carried an average as high as 182 in several seasons. Notice that she is using a conventional grip in her ball with her fingers sunk up to the first knuckle. The conventional grip is the best for most women, in my opinion, because of their lack of great hand strength. I am counseling Cherile to keep the back of her hand firm and on the outside of the ball as she makes her delivery.

180

Ethel Larson

This is an excellent head-on view of a good woman bowler, Ethel Larson, of Bloomfield Hills, Michigan. Ethel shows perfect balance here with her weight back on her right heel ready to step off with her left foot into her approach. See how she has cradled the ball in both hands to help take the weight off her bowling arm and hand. Ethel rolls a 14-pound ball and has averaged 175 for many years. The only criticism I would make of this picture of Ethel is that I would prefer to see her ball held a little more to her right side so that it drops away into its backswing without any possibility of its getting into an outside arc. Notice, too, that she is using a conventional grip in her bowling ball.

CHAPTER 24

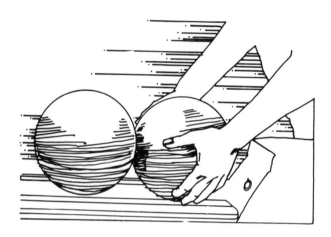

At last I am disclosed as the left-hander I truly am! Since I have been bowling all my life as a left-hander I feel that I am very well qualified to give the five to seven percent of all bowlers who are left-handed some expert advice on their "problem."

Left-handed bowlers have finally come into their own in the bowling world. Some of the best bowlers of our time are left-handed; Johnny Petraglia, Dave Davis, Bill Allen, and "Skee" Foremsky are all left-handed and champions all.

In the early days of bowling, it was an advantage to bowl left-handed because the left side of the lane was not used as much as the right, and the result was that the left-hander had almost a virgin track. At least he had a track that was fairly consistent in its conditioning as contrasted to the right-hander's track which

Bowling for Left-Handers

could vary from a well-worn one to an erratic one as a result of various lines being used on it. Most left-handed bowlers roll big hooks because they start from the far left-hand side of the lane. That angle is the simplest and best one for a left-hander to use because it will give his ball a true roll and a stronger finish at the end.

The presence of a track can be an advantage for the right-hander. But, the left-hander, who must bowl without a track worn into the lane, seems to have a wider pocket. At least, it seems to me that I have one, and I have discussed this with other left-handers, who agree with me on the subject. Anyway, there is nothing I can do about my left-handedness, nor is there anything you can do about yours. We must work with it in the same way that a right-handed bowler works with his natural ball.

I feel that I need not adjust my line as frequently as the right-handed bowler does, and as a result I believe that I can bowl more confidently knowing that the line I start with on a lane is likely to be the one I end with, subject to the usual minor corrections due to heat and dust and moisture on the lane.

All the basic fundamentals I have explained for right-handed bowlers apply equally as well to left-handed bowlers. All you have to do is translate the "right" into the "left" in my instructions. I do have this one personal bit of advice, however, and that is that I think you will need to make one board adjustment, or possibly two boards adjustment in your starting positions...*toward* the channel. You will have to find this out for yourself, but once you have, you will be a winning left-hander!

CHAPTER 25

This book has attempted to give you a sound foundation in bowling principles and theory from which you can start to develop your own distinctive bowling style. I have given you directions quite emphatically sometimes in this book, such as, "Put your target foot on the center dot," or "Bowl this or that spare from this particular angle."

Now I want to go on record once more that this bowling game is an individual game with an individual style for every bowler. You may be taller than the average bowler, or shorter than the average bowler. Therefore, please understand, that when I say, "Put your foot on the center dot," it is entirely possible that for your individual bowling it would be better for you to be six inches behind that dot (if you are tall) or six inches in front of that dot (if you are short).

Develop Your Own
Bowling Style

The best way for you to determine your starting position distance from the foul line is to reverse your approach. Start at the foul line and walk away from it toward the front of the approach in what would be your normal walking steps. Then add the distance of a half-step to account for your slide and the result will be your individual starting position within a few inches. At least, as you begin the bowling game you should start at that point consistently.

As you go along in your bowling career, don't be afraid to change your starting position, making it closer or farther away from the foul line as your game develops. Sometimes shortening your delivery by only a few inches may make a world of difference in the compactness of your delivery. Or lengthening it may allow you to get additional "steam" into your ball. Experiment with new positions and then settle down on one, whether new or not, and give yourself a chance to observe what happens as a result of a slight change. Perhaps you will adapt the revised position into your game; perhaps you won't. Let good bowling results give you the answer.

After you have begun to standardize your bowling delivery and can count on six inches or more of consistent hook at the end of your ball track, then you can depart moderately from the exact orders I have given you in this book. Nearly all the starting positions and lane angles I have outlined for you remain consistently valid in relation to one another and in relation to the various "best" angles recommended for the conversion of the spares and splits. However, if you find that you can convert the 10-pin or, for that matter, any other pin or spare by going completely contrary to the recommended angle (that is, for example, by bowling for the 10-pin from the far right position), by all means bowl for it from far right. The purpose of this game is to knock down the most pins, get the most strikes, convert the most spares and splits, and thereby get the highest total score. Remember the old adage of Lloyd Mangrum in golf, "Are we playing how or how many?" I give you permission to quote that adage to your opponents, too, when they complain, as they will, when you get a "lucky" strike.

I have instructed you in this book to make a straight approach to the foul line, and, as you know, many of the instructions are based upon the supposition that the bowler has made a straight line approach. It is possible that you, like thousands of other bowlers, find it constitutionally impossible to walk a straight line. One of the great bowlers of all time, Eddie Lubanski, of the Detroit Stroh Championship team, never walked a straight line but would slant in with his second step and then slant out on his third step in his approach to the line. Harry Smith too, another great bowler, was famous for his erratic run to the line.

So, if you find you cannot make a straight approach, don't worry about it. Work on the approach you have until you have standardized your inconsistency and then live with it. Adapt the starting positions I have designated so that they correlate with your approach style. Perhaps for you a constant correction of one board, right or left, or more will be necessary for your best bowling. My point is this—understand the theory and put it into practice, adapting the various suggestions to fit your own individual case.

Along this same line, I want to tell you a true story about an unusual and different bowler who once "murdered" one of the best teams of bowlers in America. This famous team (I won't tell you their names for fear of embarrassing them) was on an exhibition tour and got caught in a terrible snowstorm in Salt Lake City, Utah. To while away the several days until they could get back on the road, they decided to bowl in a neighborhood bowling lane. There they picked up a local bowler who bowled in most unorthodox fashion. He was a right-hander and bowled like a left-hander, that is, his approach started at the Far Right position and he ran left to deliver, right-handedly remember, the most vicious left to right hook any of those great bowlers had ever seen. He beat them soundly with a most unorthodox bowling style. These great bowlers are still shaking their heads over "what happened in Salt Lake City."

I hope that this book will encourage you to become a better bowler and I sincerely hope that this book will also help you to achieve an enviable ambition, to know what you are doing when you bowl and thus have worlds more fun in bowling!

189

Glossary

Bowling terms may vary in different localities. What follows is a guide to bowling terms in this book with a few colorful additions.

Action: Movement imparted to the ball by the fingers as the ball is released.

Anchor man: The last bowler in a team.

Angle: Direction taken by the ball as it enters the 1-3 pocket.

Arrows: Dart-like markers out on the lane 12 to 16 feet used by the bowler to help him keep his line to the pins.

Baby strike: Pins left after the first ball so that there is a pocket corresponding to the 1-3 pocket for the full setup.

Back-up ball: Ball that moves to the right, the opposite of a hook.

Blow: Fail to make a spare; technically, an error.

Break of the boards: Point approximately 16 feet out from the foul line just beyond the darts, or arrows.

Brooklyn: Ball thrown into the 1-2 pocket.

Channel: Gutter on each side of the lane.

Cherry: Pin left when a pin in front is knocked down, or chopped; a bowler who has so performed is said to have picked a cherry.

Chinaman: Third bowler in a team.

Chop: To hit a front pin and leave one or more behind it.

Crossover: Ball thrown into the 1-2 pocket; crossover line is aim of the bowler to hit this pocket.

Dump: Dropping the ball at the foul line, usually as a result of rushing the line.

Deflection: Movement of the ball from its true path caused by a pin or pins that are hit.

Die: Ball losing action or velocity at the end of a roll.

Fill: Number of pins dropped after a spare.

Flatten: To turn the wrist away from the ball at the end of the ball release.

Foul line: Line at the end of the approach marking the beginning of the lane; a sliding foot or any other part of the bowler's body touching the lane beyond the foul line results in loss of all pins made on the roll.

Frame: One of the ten divisions of a game; the corresponding box on a score sheet.

Get-away: Action of dropping the ball at the foul line; *see also* Dump.

Hang a corner pin: Leave a corner pin standing.

Headpin: The 1 pin.

Heavy: Ball that hits the 1-pin head on; *also* on the nose.

High: Head on to the headpin.

Holding lane: Lane that resists the hook motion of the ball.

Hook: Break of the ball into the 1-3 pocket.

Kickback: Side wall on each side of the pin deck.

Lay a foundation: Strike in the ninth frame.

Lead-off man: First bowler in a team.

Leave: Pins standing after the first ball of a frame.

Light hit: Ball that barely touches the 1 pin; *also* thin.

Miss: Fail to make a spare; *also* blow; an error.

Open frame: A pin or pins left standing after the second ball.

Pick a cherry: *See* Cherry.

Pie alley: Lane that allows high scores.

Pin action: Motion of struck pins that in turn knock over others.

Pin deck: Area at the end of the lane on which the pins are positioned.

Pit: The area at the end of the lane beyond the pin deck.

Pocket: Space between the 1- and 3-pins; space between 1- and 2-pins for left-handers.

Ringing-10 pin: 10-pin left standing after a powerful strike; *also* ringing 4-pin.

Running lane: Lane on which the ball hooks easily.

Side walls: Kickbacks on each side of the pin deck.

Sleeper: Pin hidden behind another in a spare.

Solid: A strong hit.

Spare: To knock down all ten pins with the first and second balls; also the score for so doing.

Split: Leave of two or more pins (not the 1-pin) with intervening space where pins have fallen.

Stiff lane: Lane that resists a hook.

Strike: To knock down all ten pins with the first ball; also the score for so doing.

Strong: Ball that has a good deal of action; *also* working.

Swishing 7-pin: 7-pin left standing as other pins swish by it; *also* swishing 10-pin.

Tap: Hit that seems perfect but leaves one pin standing.

Thin hit: *See* Light hit.

Tickler: 6-pin that bounces off the right kickback and knocks down the 10-pin.

Track: (1) the path on a bowling ball that it rolls on most often; (2) path on a bowling lane over which many bowlers roll.

Washout: The 1-2-10 spare.

Wall shot: Strike that is aided by pins coming off the left kickback to knock over other pins.

Weak 7-pin: Pin left standing after an unforceful hit; *also* weak 4-pin.

Wire it: Throw three strikes in the tenth frame.

Index